JOHN MILLS

JOHN MILLS

Robert Tanitch

COLLINS & BROWN

For John and Lynne Smithard

Also by Robert Tanitch
A Pictorial Companion to Shakespeare's Plays
Ralph Richardson, A Tribute
Olivier
Leonard Rossiter
Ashcroft
Gielgud
Dirk Bogarde
Guinness
Sean Connery

HALF TITLE PAGE John Mills in *The Way to the Stars*, 1945.
FRONTISPIECE John Mills in *Great Expectations*, 1946.

135798642

First published in Great Britain in 1993
by Collins & Brown Limited
Mercury House
195 Knightsbridge
London SW7 1RE

British Library Cataloguing-in-Publication Data:
A catalogue record for this book
is available from the British Library.

ISBN 1 85585 142 3 (hardback edition)
ISBN 1 85585 163 6 (paperback edition)

Filmset by Goodfellow & Egan

Reproduction by Daylight, Singapore

Printed and bound in Great Britain by Butler & Tanner, Frome, Somerset

Contents

Introduction 7

The Thirties 15

The Forties 47

The Fifties 69

The Sixties 99

The Seventies 121

The Eighties 137

Awards and Honours 149

Chronology 150

Acknowledgements 159

Index 160

Introduction

John Mills is one of the most popular and enduring stars of our time. This book is a pictorial record of his career in theatre, film and television from 1929 to the present day.

JOHN MILLS HAS BEEN DESCRIBED as the most English of actors. Equally adept in middle-class and working-class roles, he came to represent, for many cinemagoers, all that was best and lasting in the national character. He personified the British love of understatement and enjoyed a great success in war films. He typified the ordinary man, the boy next door, every mum's son, the serviceman doing his duty. It was important to him to get it right; he was always conscious of his responsibility to the real sailors, airmen and soldiers he was portraying. He has played these modest yet determined war heroes for so long and so often and so convincingly, with unforced naturalism and controlled emotion, that his dramatic range has been underrated.

Mills has appeared in modern plays, the classics, musicals and revues. He has acted in Shakespeare, Oliver Goldsmith, Arthur Wing Pinero, Bernard Shaw, Harold Brighouse, Somerset Maugham, John Steinbeck, André Roussin and Ray Lawler. He has created roles for Noël Coward, John Van Druten, Terence Rattigan, Mary Hayley Bell, Charles Wood, William Douglas Home and Brian Clark.

He has been cast as office boy, millionaire, cabbie, magistrate, carpenter, shopkeeper, Greek scholar, trade unionist, sheikh, master bootmaker, randy farmer, Harley Street doctor, migrant labourer, butler, Australian canecutter, lawyer, retired potter, sacked schoolteacher, private detective, Russian peasant, German spy, dustman, member of the IRA, pacifist, crook, prime minister and village idiot.

He has led his step-father astray, mistaken his future father-in-law for an innkeeper, shot his best friend, gone to prison for a crime he has not committed and been murdered in St Pancras Station.

He has also driven an ambulance across the Libyan Desert, acquired a new pair of hands, dressed up as a woman, fallen off a derrick in Texas, been beheaded in the Tower of London and put a girdle round the earth in forty minutes twice...

LEWIS ERNEST WATTS MILLS was born on 22 February 1908 at The Watts Naval Training College for Boys in Norfolk where his father was mathematics master. Not liking his Christian names, he called himself Jack and then much later, on his sister's suggestion, changed it to John.

He was educated in Suffolk at the village school in Belton and at St John Leeman School in Beccles (where he played Puck in Shakespeare's *A Midsummer Night's Dream* for the first time) before transferring to Norwich High School where he was miserable until he dealt decisively with a notorious bully, in much the same way that years later he was to deal with the spiv, played by Stewart Granger in the film, *Waterloo Road*.

At sixteen he left school to become an office boy in the Ipswich Corn Exchange. At nineteen he decided to quit and come to London to find work in the theatre. Mills had wanted to be an actor ever since he could remember, but first he had to work for six months as a commercial traveller (selling toilet paper) in order to pay the rent. He took dancing lessons and finally landed his first job in 1929 in the back row of the chorus in a musical, *The Five O'Clock Girl*, at the London Hippodrome. While the show was running he appeared in cabaret.

When the musical folded, and having attended some forty auditions and failed to find employment in the West End, he joined The Quaints on a tour of the Far East in a repertory of plays and musicals which included *Hamlet, Young Woodley* and *Mr Cinders*. 'One of the secrets of his successful performances', wrote the drama critic of *The Strait Times*, 'is the possession of that rare quality, personal charm.' It was in Singapore that he first met and acted with Noël Coward, who, holidaying abroad, recklessly agreed to stand in for an indisposed actor, playing Captain Stanhope to his Lieutenant Raleigh in R. C. Sherriff's *Journey's End. The Ceylon Times*, praising Mills's absolute naturalism, found it difficult to imagine anyone better suited to the part. In his autobiography, *Present Indicative*, Coward said he was the finest Raleigh he had ever seen.

On his return to England, he was cast in the leading role of *Charley's Aunt* (1930) and saw his name in lights for the first time. He followed Brandon Thomas's farce with *Charles Cochrane's 1931 Revue* which lasted three weeks and then appeared in John Van Druten's *London Wall*, the earliest of the cockney and semi-cockney roles with which he would come to be identified throughout his career.

Mills spent a year in Noël Coward's spectacular and immensely patriotic *Cavalcade* (1931), turning down the opportunity to re-create his part in the Hollywood movie because he wanted to stay in the theatre. Coward put him into his next revue, *Words and Music* (1932).

In 1933 he took over, at three days' notice, one of the leading roles in the musical, *Give Me a Ring*, when the Hungarian star, who had been engaged, was refused a work-permit. The show ran for a year and Mills acted with three different leading ladies: Evelyn Laye, Binnie Hale and Adele Dixon. He was then seen in the musical, *Jill Darling* (1934) which also proved very popular.

In 1936 he appeared in James Lonsdale Hodson's *Red Night* which failed (West End audiences by this time being tired of dramas about World War I) but which was, nevertheless, very good for his career in that his personal success as a British Tommy established him in the straight theatre.

A farce and three more flops followed before Tyrone Guthrie invited him to join the Old Vic Company in 1938 to play Puck in *A Midsummer Night's Dream* and Young Marlow in Oliver Goldsmith's *She Stoops to Conquer*. Guthrie wanted him to come back the following season to play

Hamlet, Richard III and Hotspur in *Henry IV Part 1*, but World War II put a stop to that. It is interesting to think that had Mills returned to the Old Vic, his career would almost certainly have been in theatre rather than in films.

He was in *We at the Crossroads* (1939), a dull and pretentious drama by Keith Winter, which owed something to J. M. Barrie's *Dear Brutus*. Much more worthwhile was John Steinbeck's *Of Mice and Men* (1939), performed initially at a club theatre because it had been banned by the censor on account of the bad language. Under pressure from the Press, the Lord Chamberlain was forced to relent and the production transferred to the West End where it would have had a long run had it not been for the war and the closing of all the theatres. Mills's characterization, modelled on James Cagney, was admired for its charm, conviction and nervous tension.

On the outbreak of hostilities he enlisted immediately, served in the Royal Engineers, was commissioned in 1941 and invalided out in 1942. His first job in the theatre was a Resistance thriller, *Men in Shadow*, written by his wife, Mary Hayley Bell, who would also write *Duet for Two Hands* for him, a piece of grand guignol, which enjoyed a long run in 1945. He gained excellent reviews in Tyrone Guthrie's expressionistic *Top of the Ladder* (1950), but his excellence was not enough to save the play. He had better luck with André Roussin's comedy, *Figure of Fun* (1951) and a revival of *Charley's Aunt* (1954), throwing himself into the farce with such energy that he lost nearly a stone in weight. He also acted in Mary Hayley Bell's *The Uninvited Guest* (1953), the critics showing far more interest in his wig than they did in the plot.

Mills made his Broadway début in 1961 as T. E. Lawrence in Terence Rattigan's *Ross*, scoring a big critical success. He was not seen on the London stage again until two years later, and then only briefly, in *Power of Persuasion*, Gert Hofmann's parable on the German Socialist Party. Nine years later, he joined John Gielgud at the Royal Court in Charles Wood's film satire, *Veterans*, and then was cast as the Labour Prime Minister in William Douglas Home's political comedy, *At the End of the Day*.

Mills has described the musical version of J. B. Priestley's *The Good Companions* (1974) as one of the happiest times he has spent in the theatre. The unexpected sight of him, at sixty-six years old, singing and dancing a complicated tap routine, stopped the show, taking the first-night audience completely by surprise, most of them being far too young to know that he had begun his career as a hoofer. He followed this musical with another, *Great Expectations* (1975), playing Joe Gargery, which did not come into London, and then appeared in a revival of Terence Rattigan's *Separate Tables* (1977) in which he was most moving as a bogus major.

He played the title role in a musical version of *Goodbye Mr Chips* (1982) at the Chichester Festival Theatre and the title role in an over-free adaptation of Arthur Wing Pinero's *The Magistrate* called *Little Lies* (1983). His performance as a blinkered Tory reactionary in Charles Clark's *The Petition* (1986) at the National Theatre ranks among his best and was much admired by his peers. His most recent stage role has been Alfred Doolittle in a revival of Bernard Shaw's *Pygmalion* (1987) in New York, opposite Peter O'Toole. In his eighty-fifth year he is still treading the boards in his one-man show, *An Evening with John Mills*.

J OHN MILLS MADE HIS FILM début in 1932 in *The Midshipmaid*, singing and dancing opposite Jessie Matthews. For the next four years he appeared mainly in quota quickies, all mediocre and instantly forgettable. The films paid the rent, but they did not give him the acting opportunities many critics felt he deserved.

His most important role was the lead in *Brown on Resolution* (1935, later retitled *Forever England*), which won him a two-year contract. The parts did not improve until 1942 when Noël Coward produced *In Which We Serve*, creating 'Shorty' Blake specially for him. The film was a major turning-point in his career. Shorty, the working-class hero, transparently decent and honest, would turn up again with subtle differences in *This Happy Breed* (1944) and *Waterloo Road* (1945).

The first time he was cast as an officer was in 1943 in *We Dive at Dawn*. British Studios would go on refighting World War II well into the 1960s and, because war heroes were often the only roles on offer (British actresses used to complain bitterly that there were no parts for them), it must have seemed to cinemagoers, and indeed to Mills himself, that he would never lose his stiff-upper-lip.

His outstanding films during this period were Terence Rattigan's *The Way to the Stars* (1945), a beautifully understated and deeply moving remembrance of the Battle of Britain, and David Lean's definitive version of *Great Expectations* (1946), which made him an international

star. He also appeared as the doctor in *So Well Remembered* (1947), the murder suspect in *The October Man* (1947) and the title role in *Scott of the Antarctic* (1948), an immensely worthy but finally bland tribute which missed the greatness at which it aimed.

Mills then went into production on his own account, but when *The History of Mr Polly* (a film of which he had every right to be proud) and *The Rocking Horse Winner* both failed at the box office in 1949, he decided to stick to acting.

The enormous success of *Morning Departure* (1950), in which he gave a performance notable for its realism, tact and inner power, was a classic example of his style and technical skill and would lead to *The Colditz Story* (1955 – 'He was', *The Times* critic wrote, 'the spirit of escape personified'), *Above Us the Waves* (1955), *Dunkirk* (1958), *Ice Cold in Alex* (1958), which surprised everybody by winning the first prize at the Berlin Film Festival, and *I Was Monty's Double* (1958), a retelling of one of World War II's famous hoaxes.

One of Mills's most celebrated and favourite roles was Willie Mossop in Harold Brighouse's *Hobson's Choice* (1954). He was not in fact David Lean's first choice and was only cast when Robert Donat fell ill just as filming was about to begin. He was immensely likeable as the timid bootmaker, who against the odds makes good.

During the Fifties he made a number of thrillers: *Mr Denning Drives North* (1951), *The Gentle Gunman* (1952). *The Long Memory* (1953), *Town on Trial* (1957) and *Vicious Circle* (1957). He also made a number of comedies: *Escapade* (1955), *It's Great to be Young* (1956) and *The Baby and the Battleship* (1956). Mills himself has dismissed many of these films as rent and tax jobs, often having to remind interviewers and

John Mills makes his West End début in the musical, *The Five O'Clock Girl*, at the London Hippodrome in 1929. The reader will have no difficulty in recognizing him.

reporters that an actor, with a family to bring up and support, has to press on with whatever comes along in order to keep the money coming in to pay the bills.

He enlivened *The End of the Affair* (1955) with his performance as the comically pathetic private detective. He played the peasant Platon in the American version of *War and Peace* (1956) and then appeared briefly, as did everybody else, in Mike Todd's spot-the-star spectacular, *Around the World in 80 Days* (1956). However, the film which had the most impact and a special place for him was the unpretentious and very appealing thriller, *Tiger Bay* (1959), in which his young daughter, Hayley Mills, became a star overnight.

Mills played opposite Alec Guinness in *Tunes of Glory* (1960), taking the acting prize at the Venice Film Festival for his performance as the rigid martinet who gradually cracks up. He followed this first-rate melodrama with adaptations of two stage plays: Ray Lawler's Australian drama, *The Summer of the Seventeenth Doll* (1960) and Ted Willis's *Flame in the Streets* (1962), a British working-class *Guess Who's Coming to Dinner?*

He was the priest in *The Singer Not the Song* (1961), a gay western whose soul, despite its location work in Spain, remained firmly in Pinewood. He played the humiliated pip-squeak in the class-war comedy, *Tiara Tahiti* (1962), opposite James Mason, and he was very funny as the fratricide elder brother in *The Wrong Box* (1965).

His partnership with Hayley continued in *The Swiss Family Robinson* (1960), *The Chalk Garden* (1964), *The Truth About Spring* (1965) and *Sky West and Crooked* (1965) which he directed. Best of all was Bill Naughton's *The Family Way* (1967). His portrait of the belt-and-braces, collarless-shirted, Lawrentian-moustached, beer-swilling North Country dad was a splendid late example of the Manchester school of sentimental realism, comic yet sad.

There were more war films. The first was *The Valiant* (1962) in which he looked understandably worried with a time-bomb ticking away under his destroyer. The second was *King Rat* (1965), perhaps Bryan Forbes's best film and long overdue for reappraisal. The third was the ludicrous all-star caper, *Operation Crossbow* (1965).

Two Westerns, *Chuka* (1967) and *Africa – Texas Style* (1967) were followed by the modest and infinitely superior *Run Wild, Run Free* (1969), a perfect tear-jerker for children and parents alike.

Mills acquired the film rights of *Oh! What a Lovely War* (1969) and had been working on the script with Len Deighton for several months when the Inland Revenue forced him to abandon all thoughts of directing the production and accept a television series in America. The failure of the series meant that he was able to appear in the film, which was now directed by Richard Attenborough. His unforgettable portrayal of Field Marshal Haig, sacrificing up to 50,000 men a day, remains one of his finest. He was then seen as Sir William Hamilton in *Emma Hamilton*, a German-made film, frankly more navel than naval and known in the trade as 'Carry On Emma'.

Probably the role for which Mills is best known internationally is Michael Day, the village idiot in David Lean's *Ryan's Daughter* (1970). The character was so powerful that it threatened to take over the production and at one stage there was even talk of calling the film *Michael Day*. Mills won an Oscar, but the critics were by no means unanimous in their praise, some regrettably unable to see any further than the make-up.

Since then, he has appeared mainly in cameo parts in such epics as *Young Winston* (1971), *Lady Caroline Lamb* (1972), *Zulu Dawn* (1978), *Gandhi* (1981) and remakes of *The Big Sleep* (1978) and *The Thirty-Nine Steps* (1978). His most substantial roles have been the dirty old farmer in love with a buxom wench in *Dulcima* (1971), the reformed ne'er-do-well in the oil drama, *Oklahoma Crude* (1973) and the Vatican priest in *The Devil's Advocate* (1977).

He has also appeared as a sheikh in *Sahara* (1983), a film inspired by the misadventures of Mark Thatcher in the desert, and as an eccentric millionaire in the Madonna vehicle, *Who's That Girl?*

MILLS MADE HIS TELEVISION début live in America in 1956 in a production of Somerset Maugham's *The Letter*. It was not, he said, an experience he wished to repeat.

In the 1960s he starred in *Dundee and the Culhane*, a Western series which he hoped would launch his career in the United States, but which unfortunately did nothing of the sort, coming to an abrupt halt after only a few weeks.

In the 1970s, he was seen as a busker in *The Nanny and the Professor*, opposite his daughter Hayley, and as a waning sorcerer in *Dr Strange*. He did not make his British début until 1978 when he donned so many disguises in the serial *The Zoo Gang* that even the television crew failed to recognize him. A much-heralded revival of *Quatermass* (1979) proved something of an anti-climax.

In the 1980s he acted in three *Tales of the Unexpected*, an Agatha Christie murder mystery, a Sherlock Holmes murder mystery (playing Dr Watson), two adaptations of Barbara Taylor Bradford, a pilot for *The Adventures of Little Lord Fauntleroy* and, most popular of all, the Darby and Jones series, *Young at Heart*.

He has also appeared in the Australian children's classic, *Spit McPhee* (1988), the Anglo-French production of *A Tale of Two Cities* (1989 – playing the lawyer, Mr Lorry), Kingsley Amis's tragic farce, *Ending Up* (1990), in which, cast against type, he was excellent and *Night of the Fox* (1990). His most recent roles have been in *Perfect Scoundrels* (1992), *Frankenstein, The Real Story* (1993) and *Harnessing Peacocks* (1993).

JOHN MILLS, RELIABLE AND CONSISTENT as an actor, is a great survivor. The pages which follow are a pictorial record of his career, a reminder of his charm, integrity, versatility, professionalism and perennial youth. They are also a tribute to the man himself and the contribution he has made to the British cinema and theatre over six decades.

The Thirties

Charley's Aunt • 1930
A play by Brandon Thomas, directed by Amy Brandon Thomas at New Theatre.

At twenty-one, Mills was the youngest actor ever to play Lord Fancourt Babberley on the West End stage.

'Babs', an undergraduate up at Oxford in 1892, was persuaded by his university chums to impersonate Charley's rich aunt from Brazil (where the nuts come from). They needed an elderly and respectable lady to chaperon their girlfriends. Babs then found himself having to fend off the advances of elderly gentlemen.

Twenty-four years later Mills would act this most famous of drag roles at the same theatre in a production by John Gielgud.

Mr John Mills made a very good aunt and mingled the young man and the old woman with so much ingenuity that it was agreeable to watch his skill.
The Times

Mr John Mills, as Lord Fancourt, has none of the tricks of the tired comedian, but has instead an appealing sense of fun. He leads the youthful contingent attractively.
W.A. Darlington *Daily Telegraph*

London Wall • 1931
A play by John Van Druten, directed by Auriol Lee at Duke of York's Theatre.

The setting for John Van Druten's slice-of-life drama was a typical London solicitor's office. Mills scored a big success as a cheerful and dirty-minded office boy who enjoyed reading the correspondence in the more sensational divorce cases.

Mr John Mills, as the office boy, is the very imp of vivacity and soapless squalor, perfect in collar, tie, socks and especially coiffure. His hair gives a magnificent performance.
Ivor Brown *Observer*

He was so much the real thing that I've a fancy he must be a real office boy, abducted from Fenchurch Street during the lunch hour.
Harris Deans *Illustrated Sporting and Dramatic News*

OPPOSITE An old photograph of John Mills and Arthur P. Bell in *Charley's Aunt* from John Mills's private collection.

ABOVE Helen Goss, Nadine Marsh and John Mills in *London Wall*.

Cavalcade • 1931
A play by Noël Coward, directed by Noël Coward at Theatre Royal, Drury Lane.

Cavalcade, a spectacular and patriotic pageant with a cast of over 400 actors, traced the lives of one family and its servants from the Boer War to the 1920s. 'I hope,' said Noël Coward in his curtain speech, 'that this play has made you feel, that, in spite of the troublesome times we live in, it is still pretty exciting to be English.'

Mills played the youngest son of the house, a subaltern who was killed in World War I. He had two effective scenes: the first with his girlfriend in a restaurant; the second with his mother in a moving farewell at a railway station.

The first night very nearly ended in disaster when early on in the first act, during a complicated scene change, one of the hydraulic lifts jammed and the show was held up for four and a half minutes. Coward would later describe the first night as the most agonizing three hours he had ever spent in a theatre.

Words and Music • 1932
A revue by Noël Coward, directed by Noël Coward at Adelphi Theatre.

Mills, seen here in a sketch entitled 'Children's Hour', played one of three ultra-modern children who used their rocking horse as a cocktail cabinet.

OPPOSITE Steffi Duna, Doris Hare and John Mills in *Words and Music*.

BELOW The beach of a popular seaside resort in 1910. A scene from *Cavalcade*. John Mills is on the far left of the picture.

19

The Midshipmaid • 1932
A film directed by Albert de Courville
US title: *Midshipmaid Gob*

The Midshipmaid was a comedy about a pompous economy expert visiting the Fleet in Malta, accompanied by his daughter. All the sailors fell in love with her. The film had musical interludes and Mills, cast as one of the midshipmen, sang and danced with Jessie Matthews.

Britannia of Billingsgate • 1933
A film directed by Sinclair Hill

Britannia of Billingsgate was the story of a fried-fish proprietress who became a film star. She was played by the popular cockney actress Violet Lorraine. Mills was cast as her son.

BELOW Violet Lorraine, John Mills and Glennis Lorimer in *Britannia of Billingsgate*.

OPPOSITE John Mills and Jessie Matthews in *The Midshipmaid*.

The Ghost Camera • 1933
A film directed by Bernard Vorhaus

The Ghost Camera, described as a mystery narrative, was a typical quota quickie, dashed off by the British Film industry. Bernard Vorhaus and his editor, David Lean, occasionally rose above the material, but there was little they could do with the silly toff who turned amateur sleuth.

Mills played the murder suspect and he had one good scene in the courtroom when he was being cross-examined by the coroner, played by Felix Aylmer. The photograph shows Henry Kendall, in his role of amateur sleuth, leaping to his defence.

The Lash • 1934
A film directed by Henry Edwards

The Lash was an old-fashioned melodrama in which an old-fashioned father, a self-made millionaire, dealt with his wayward son in the only way he knew how – by giving him the sound, old-fashioned thrashing he deserved. Lyn Harding played the father. Mills played the son.

The River Wolves • 1934
A film directed by George Pearson

John Mills played a young man who was being blackmailed by a gang of crooks in this waterfront melodrama down at Tilbury Docks.

ABOVE John Mills, Henry Kendall and Felix Aylmer in *The Ghost Camera*.

FAR LEFT John Mills and Lyn Harding in *The Lash*.

LEFT John Mills and Helga Moray in *The River Wolves*.

Those Were the Days • 1934
A film directed by Thomas Bentley

In the same way that Georges Feydeau is the perfect mirror to la belle époque and the naughty Nineties, so is Arthur Wing Pinero the perfect mirror to Victorian propriety and decorum. *Those Were the Days* was based on the most popular of all Pinero's stage farces, *The Magistrate*. Strictly speaking, the director spent far too much time on a loving re-creation of the English music hall when he should have been getting on with the plot.

Will Hay, in his screen début as the magistrate who was led astray by his step-son, made little attempt to act Posket, preferring to fall back on his stage comic *persona*, to the detriment of the role and the play.

The critic of the *Morning Post* was so convinced by Mills's performance, as the precocious step-son, that he actually thought he *was* a boy actor. Fifty years later Mills would play Posket in the West End.

Jill Darling • 1934
A musical by Marriott Edgar, Desmond Carter and Vivian Ellis, directed by William Mollison at Saville Theatre.

Jill Darling was the musical in which John Mills and Louise Browne sang the show-stopping 'I'm on a See-Saw'. His engaging performance was much admired for its grace, vigour and humour.

Mr Mills, in particular, should have an alluring future if some visiting film panjandrum casts a Californian eye on him.

Alan Bott *Tatler*

ABOVE Will Hay, John Mills and H. F. Maltby in *Those Were the Days*.

OPPOSITE Frances Day, Louise Browne and John Mills in *Jill Darling*.

OVERLEAF Louise Browne and John Mills singing 'I'm on a See-Saw' in *Jill Darling*.

Brown on Resolution • 1935
A film directed by Walter Forde
Retitled: *Forever England*
US titles: *Born to Glory* and *Torpedo Raider*

Brown on Resolution was made with the full co-operation of the Admiralty. It was, in fact, the very first time in the history of the British cinema that permission for the Royal Navy to be used in a fictional film had been granted.

C. S. Forester's novel describes an act of heroism on Resolution Island in the Galapagos during World War I. Able Seaman Brown, a Survivor of *HMS Rutland*, is picked up by the German battleship *Zeithen*. He manages to escape and single-handed delays her vital repairs for twelve decisive hours by sniping at her riveters.

The story was told in a simple and almost documentary manner, without jingoism and false heroics, showing compassion for both the British and the Germans. The climax, vividly photo-graphed, was so spectacular and exciting that many critics felt the film would have been better without the lengthy domestic scenes which led to Brown's birth.

Mills's performance, unforced and modest, was a study of blind, dogged and boyish patriotism. The film was a major turning-point in his career.

Brown, who matters more than anyone else in the picture, is perfectly cast.

Sunday Times

Mr John Mills – except when he fails to control his Oxford accent – is excellent as Brown.

Charles Davy *Spectator*

The acting of John Mills as Brown lifts him at a stride into the ranks of the stars.

Campbell Dixon *Daily Telegraph*

I am a bit on the short side for romantic parts. What I would like to be is an English James Cagney.

John Mills quoted by Jympson Harman
Evening News

LEFT John Mills in *Brown on Resolution*.

Car of Dreams • 1935
A film directed by Graham Cutts and Austin Melford

Car of Dreams was a light-hearted farcical romance set in a musical instrument factory. Mills played a poor little rich boy, son of the owner of the factory, who fell in love with a girl who worked in his father's office. He made her a present of a Rolls-Royce, posing as its chauffeur.

Given a good part here he shows that he has the early makings of the sort of bright and cheery young leading man that we lack so much in our films.
Philip Page Sunday Referee

He's that rare commodity in British Studios – a personable young man who can sing and dance, and play comedy, without loss of virility. To borrow the pet phrase of an eminent statesman, he will probably go up and up and up and on and on and on.
John K. Newman Film Weekly

The white Rolls-Royce stole the film.
John Mills Up in the Clouds, Gentlemen Please

LEFT Grete Mosheim and John Mills in *Car of Dreams*.

BELOW John Mills and June Clyde in *Charing Cross Road*.

Charing Cross Road • 1935
A film directed by Albert de Courville

John Mills and American actress June Clyde were cast as two young lovers in search of stardom and agreeing not to marry until they had found it.

First Offence • 1936
A film directed by Herbert Mason
US title: Bad Blood

A wealthy French doctor, fed up with his son's bad behaviour, sold the luxury car he had given him. The son stole the car from the new owners and joined a gang of car thieves. Mills played the son and Lilli Palmer played his girlfriend.

John Mills as Johnnie makes a pleasant manly type of young hero.
Picture Show

John Mills is probably one of the cleverest drivers on the screen; and in this picture he is given ample scope for his talents as a speed ace.
Observer

BELOW Bernard Nedell and John Mills in *First Offence*.

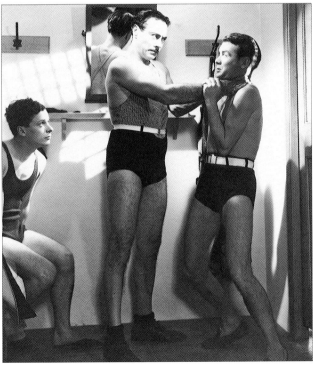

Red Night • 1936
A play by James Lansdale Hodson, directed by Miles Malleson at Queen's Theatre.

Red Night marked Robert Donat's first venture as an actor-manager. On its pre-London tour, it was obvious to everybody that his role was much inferior to the role Mills was playing and he was strongly advised not to bring the play into the West End. However, with characteristic generosity, Donat ignored the advice.

James Lansdale Hodson's sincere yet sentimental document of life in the trenches during World War I was not another *Journey's End* and the play failed.

The play centres round Private Summers, the epitome of the Cockney Tommy, a full-length portrait faithfully delineated. Mr John Mills gives a superb performance and is Private Summers to the life.

New Statesman and Nation

Mr John Mills gives a brilliant performance as the Cockney; not the least merit of his acting is his firm control of a part which, over-exuberantly played, would have upset the balance of the play.

Peter Fleming *Spectator*

Aren't Men Beasts! • 1936
A play by Vernon Sylvaine, directed by Leslie Henson at Strand Theatre.

Aren't Men Beasts! was a vehicle for Robertson Hare who played a dentist who had been accused of assault and suffered every kind of indignity. Mills was cast as his son.

John Mills is one of the best of our young actors – equally at home in straight or musical comedy or drama.

Philip Page *Daily Mail*

ABOVE Robert Donat and John Mills in *Red Night*.

OPPOSITE John Mills and Jean Ormonde in *Aren't Men Beasts!*

Tudor Rose • 1936
A film directed by Robert Stevenson
US title: *Nine Days a Queen*

Tudor Rose was the story of Lady Jane Grey, who was beheaded by Mary Tudor. The theatrical fiction, poorly scripted, was given a distinguished theatrical cast which included Gwen Ffrangcon-Davies, Cedric Hardwicke, Felix Aylmer, Sybil Thorndike, Martita Hunt, Miles Malleson and Frank Cellier.

Nova Pilbeam played Jane Grey and Mills played Dudley, son of the Earl of Warwick, who married her and was also beheaded.

John Mills gives his most attractive performance as Lord Guildford.

News Chronicle

This sentimental pageant in fancy dress could have displayed no more ignorance of the period had it been made in Hollywood.

Graham Greene *Spectator*

O.H.M.S. • 1936
A film directed by Raoul Walsh
US title: *You're in the Army Now*

O.H.M.S., a comedy drama set in the British regular army in peacetime, was made primarily to stimulate recruiting. The leading role was taken by the American actor Wallace Ford. He played a small-time crook (with a big sense of humour) who fled to England and died a hero's death while fighting marauding bandits in China. Mills was cast as an honest lance-corporal, his rival for the favours of the sergeant-major's daughter.

OPPOSITE John Mills and Nova Pilbeam in *Tudor Rose*.

BELOW Wallace Ford and John Mills in *O. H. M. S.*

Floodlight • 1937
**A revue by Beverley Nichols, directed by
C. Denis Freeman at Saville Theatre.**

The critics enjoyed the charm and vivacity of Mills,
but on the whole they thought Beverley Nichols
should stick to gardening.

*He has versatility, good looks, and a charmingly
unspoiled personality, and even if he never achieves
Covent Garden he will always be able to evoke
shrill hysterics from the gallery girls.*
                    Stanley Parker *Illustrated Sporting and
                                    Dramatic News*

*Revue, say the pessimists, has been dying for a
number of years. Having seen Mr Nichols'*
Floodlight, *I can only say that if this is a sample of
what we are to expect from one of the leading
writers of the day, then the sooner revue dies and is
decently buried the better.*
                    David Fairweather *Theatre World*

The Green Cockatoo • 1937
**A film directed by William Cameron Menzies
US title: *Four Dark Hours***

The Green Cockatoo was the British film industry's
feeble attempt to make an American-style gangster
movie and cash in on the public's interest in the
police campaign against London's underworld.

Mills was a cocky little tough guy, in a pin-stripe
suit, who made his living as a cabaret entertainer at
The Green Cockatoo, a sleazy joint in Soho. The
role called for him to wisecrack, sing, dance, use his
fists and imitate James Cagney. The wisecracking
was pretty awful. The most enjoyable moments
were when he tap-danced and sang 'Smokey Joe'.

The film was not released in England until 1939.

ABOVE Frances Day and John Mills in *Floodlight*.

OPPOSITE René Ray and John Mills in *The Green Cockatoo*.

36

Pélissier's Follies • 1938
A musical entertainment directed by Anthony Pélissier at Saville Theatre.

Pélissier's Follies was an attempt to revive the *Follies* of old; but although the actors did occasionally wear pierrot costume, the show was much nearer to a revue than a concert party. The photograph on the left is of a sketch called 'What Use is the Seaside?', a comment on staggered holidays which had a pay-off line the critic of *Theatre World* could not bring himself to repeat.

John Mills's crooning waiter is a cruel, beautifully observed picture of Levantine effrontery.
James Agate *Sunday Times*

ABOVE John Mills and Doris Hare in *Pélissier's Follies*.

LEFT John Mills and Roma Beaumont in *Pélissier's Follies*.

RIGHT John Mills in *Pélissier's Follies*.

A Midsummer Night's Dream • 1938

A play by William Shakespeare, directed by Tyrone Guthrie at Old Vic Theatre.

Tyrone Guthrie's tuppence-coloured production, with music by Mendelssohn and scenery by Oliver Messell, was a most rare vision: the Elizabethan Age seen through Victorian eyes. Mills's merry wanderer of the night was as impudent and as naughty a Puck as anybody could have wished.

Mr John Mills charmingly presents a Puck as fresh and pliant as a sapling and adds the pounce of a cat.
Ivor Brown *Observer*

RIGHT Ruth Wynn-Owen, Anthony Nicholls, Harry Andrews, Peggy Livesey, John Mills, and Robert Helpmann in *A Midsummer Night's Dream*.

She Stoops to Conquer • 1939
A play by Oliver Goldsmith, directed by Esme Church at Old Vic Theatre.

She Stoops to Conquer, a sentimental, good-humoured and beautifully constructed eighteenth-century comedy, is among the most popular plays in the English language.

Mills played Young Marlow, the bashful hero who, having mistaken a country house for an inn, is mortified to learn that the landlord he has been insulting is his future father-in-law and the barmaid he has been trying to bed is the girl he has come down to court.

Mr John Mills – tenor rather than baritone in volume – plays Young Marlow delightfully.

Harold Hobson *Observer*

He has a dash and impudence and a good swaggering presence but there is nothing better in his playing of the part than the display of tongue-tied embarrassment and diffidence with which he first confronts Miss Hardcastle.

A. E. Wilson *Star*

Mr John Mills makes a graceful and dashing if here and there a slightly too facetious and up-to-date Marlow.

New Statesman and Nation

OPPOSITE John Mills and Ursula Jeans in *She Stoops to Conquer*.

BELOW George Benson, Margaret Yarde, Frank Napier, Edward Chapman, Ursula Jeans, John Mills, Pamela Brown and Anthony Nicholls in *She Stoops to Conquer*.

Of Mice and Men • 1939
A play by John Steinbeck, directed by Norman Marshall at Gate Theatre (the production transferred to the Apollo Theatre).

John Steinbeck's modern classic, a powerful and moving story of two migrant labourers, is set during the American Depression, when up to 15 million people were out of work.

Nial MacGinnis played the stupid, childlike Lennie, a huge man, unaware of his frightening strength. Mills was cast as George, who both protected and used him, spending their hard-earned money on drink, gambling and the whorehouse, when he should have been saving it for their dream farm. The closing moments of the play, when George killed Lennie before the lynch-mob could get him, were particularly impressive.

If John Mills, whom I have seen in a short space of time in revue, musical comedy, farce and classic comedy, is not one of the most versatile actors of the day, then I have no notion what acting is.
A. E. Wilson *Star*

There was a performance by Mr John Mills for sheer, quick, honest virtuosity which would be hard to beat.
Lionel Hale *News Chronicle*

Mr John Mills, who is a great little master of pathos, and in addition has the gift possessed by few actors of simultaneously leading an outer and an inner life.
Richard Prentice *John O'London Weekly*

Here is another young actor on whose previous admirable work this performance of shrewdness, subtlety and pathos sets the seal.
James Agate *Sunday Times*

Goodbye Mr Chips • 1939
A film directed by Sam Wood

James Hilton's novel, a sentimental tear-jerker, was billed as 'a cavalcade of British youth'. The actors cast as the youth were pretty unconvincing and Robert Donat's Oscar-winning performance as the shy and much-loved schoolmaster (a quaint, old stick-in-the-mud) was a caricature of Chips.

Mills had the tiny part of a former pupil who asked him to look after his wife and baby while he was away at the front during World War I, where he was predictably killed.

OPPOSITE John Mills in *Of Mice and Men*.

BELOW John Mills and Robert Donat in *Goodbye Mr Chips*.

The Forties

OPPOSITE John Mills in *Scott of the Antarctic*, 1948.

All Hands • 1940
A film directed by John Paddy Carstairs

All Hands was part of the anti-gossip campaign launched by the Ministry of Information. The ten-minute film illustrated the danger of careless talk to naval men.

Old Bill and Son • 1941
A film by Ian Dalrymple

A father and son joined up. The son captured a whole platoon of German soldiers and allowed his dad, a veteran of World War I, to share the credit. The film, sentimental and unsophisticated, was based on the cartoon characters of Bruce Bairnsfather.

John Mills – one of our most neglected British artists – is very good. He avoids the high falutin' speech which is so characteristic of so many juvenile leads and plays the role of the man who is not so keen on war but sees where his duty lies with an obvious straightforward directness.

Picturegoer

A pity to see so fine an actor as John Mills in so empty a part.

Sunday Express

ABOVE Leueen McGrath and John Mills in *All Hands*.
BELOW John Mills and Morland Graham in *Old Bill and Son*.
OPPOSITE John Mills and George Cole in *Cottage to Let*.

Cottage to Let • 1941
A film directed by Anthony Asquith
US title: *Bombsight Stolen*

A Fifth Column organization kidnapped Britain's finest scientific brain with the intention of taking him to Berlin to work for Nazi Germany. The film was loosely based on a popular West End comedy-thriller. What little suspense there was suggested that the scriptwriter and the director had watched some old Alfred Hitchcock movies.

Mills's fans were not pleased to find him cast as a German spy disguised as a wounded RAF pilot. It was not much of a part until the final sequence when, during a garden fête, he was able to reveal the spy's true vicious nature, shoot his way out of an auction, and die a dirty Hun's death in a hall of mirrors.

The film is chiefly interesting now for the remarkably confident screen début of twelve-year-old George Cole, repeating his stage performance as a bright cockney evacuee who turns amateur sleuth.

The Young Mr Pitt • 1942
A film directed by Carol Reed

The Young Mr Pitt was a clever bit of propaganda, produced during the dark days of World War II when Britain stood all alone. William Pitt (as Benjamin Disraeli had been before him in the John Gielgud film, *The Prime Minister*) was dragged out of retirement to make long speeches, justifying the war. The parallels between Napoleon and Hitler were underlined. The balance between the nation's jingoism (reluctant, of course) and her deep longing for peace was finely judged. The speeches were all authentic and Robert Donat delivered the political rhetoric with considerable style.

The whole cast looked as if they might have sat for James Gilray, the eighteenth-century caricaturist. Mills played Pitt's lifelong friend, William Wilberforce.

Men in Shadow • 1942
A play by Mary Hayley Bell, directed by John Mills and Bernard Miles at Vaudeville Theatre.

Mills appeared in his wife's first play, a topical and gripping war story set in Occupied France. He was cast as the intrepid leader of a group of English saboteurs hiding in the loft of a disused mill.

RIGHT Robert Donat and John Mills in *The Young Mr Pitt*.

BELOW Derek Elphinstone and John Mills in *Men in Shadow*.

In Which We Serve • 1942
A film directed by Noël Coward and David Lean

In Which We Serve, a timely morale booster and patriotic tribute to a nation's endurance and self-sacrifice, was described by Noël Coward as the most serious and sincere job he had ever attempted.

The film, inspired by the wartime career of Lord Louis Mountbatten and dedicated to the Royal Navy, told the story of a destroyer, from the laying of its keel to it being torpedoed and sinking off Crete. The script, in a series of flashbacks, concentrated on the shore lives of three of its men: the Captain (Noël Coward), the Chief Petty Officer (Bernard Miles) and a naval rating (John Mills).

The rating was specially written for Mills. 'Shorty' Blake was every mum's son, the boy next door, quietly heroic, standing by the guns when most of the crew had been knocked out. ('Somebody had to do it.') There was one characteristic moment when Shorty was listening to Winston Churchill on the radio, telling the nation they were at war with Germany. 'You can imagine what a bitter blow it is to me,' the Prime Minister was saying. 'It isn't exactly a Bank Holiday for us,' said Shorty, speaking (as Mills was to do so often in his war films) for the nation.

In Which We Serve, in its visual authenticity, graphic staging and sharp editing, had a documentary integrity and emotional truth. The cast included Celia Johnson, Kathleen Harrison, Richard Attenborough, Joyce Carey and baby Juliet Mills, making her film début.

There can be no doubt that In Which We Serve *is the best film yet made about the war in any country.*
Edgar Anstey *Spectator*

RIGHT Vida Hope, Kay Walsh and John Mills in *In Which We Serve.*

The Black Sheep of Whitehall • 1942

A film directed by Will Hay and Basil Dearden

The Black Sheep of Whitehall was wartime slapstick. Will Hay was cast as a principal of a bankrupt correspondence course. With the help of his only pupil (John Mills), he outwitted some Nazi agents. The dialogue, the jokes, the comic routines were the pure corn of the music hall stage.

Hay was seen in a number of disguises, including a formidable nurse. He was, perhaps, at his funniest when he was mistaken for a distinguished economist and was interviewed by the BBC. Mills, in his role of straight man, was allowed his comic turn when he was pretending to be a patient suffering from amnesia.

There is also Johnny Mills, a tough, gifted, adaptable player who helps every film in which he appears. Some day some Hollywood director will 'discover' Johnny Mills and exploit a fact we have consistently over-looked – that for fifteen years we have been harbouring a British Cagney.

C. A. Lejeune *Observer*

BELOW John Mills, Will Hay and Margaret Halstan in *The Black Sheep of Whitehall*.

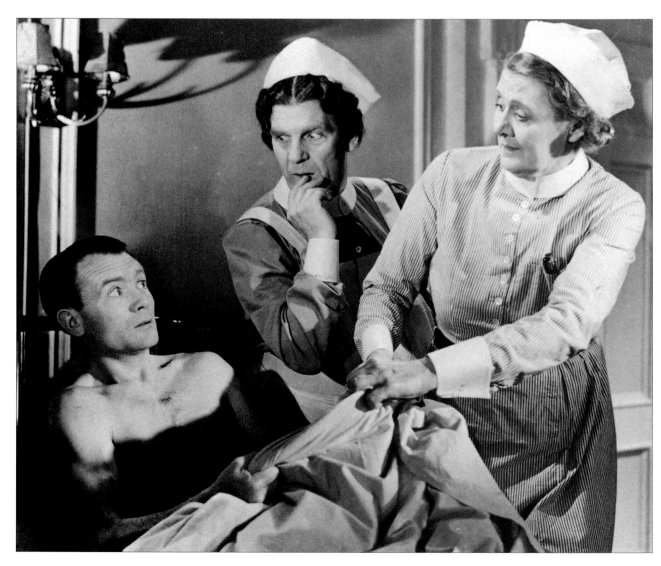

We Dive at Dawn • 1943
A film directed by Anthony Asquith

We Dive at Dawn, a wartime propaganda piece, made with the co-operation of the Admiralty, described the sinking of a German battleship by a British submarine.

The film invited unfavourable comparisons with *In Which We Serve*, in whose wake it followed. The documentary element – the stalking of the battleship, the steering of the submarine through a minefield, the behaviour of the men under fire – was fine and admirably tense in a stiff British upper lip sort of way. It was the fiction back home and Eric Portman's single-handed heroics on a foreign land which were so unconvincing.

Mills, as the Captain, was a master of controlled emotion, and the scene in which he thanks the men for their loyalty and help was perfect in its understatement.

His nervous impatience as he crouches at the periscope to manoeuvre for the attack on a battleship is a welcome change from those cinema portraits which make British officers look like bored cucumbers.

Paul Trench *Evening Standard*

John Mills (remarkable, also, it will be remembered in a sharply contrasting part in In Which We Serve*) is emerging as an actor with a special flair for realistic portrayals.*

Edgar Anstey *Spectator*

ABOVE John Mills, Norman Williams, Eric Portman and Jack Watling in *We Dive at Dawn*.

This Happy Breed • 1944
A film directed by David Lean

This Happy Breed, a suburban cavalcade, caught the imagination of suburbia and did excellent business. The screenplay, based on Noël Coward's play of the same name, traced the national events of the inter-war years through the lives of a lower-middle-class family.

The film was highly praised for its technical merits, its attention to detail, its discriminating use of technicolour and its observations of ordinary behaviour. There were some critics who put it in the same class as *Millions Like Us* and *The Way Ahead*. However, there were many people who, while not denying its warmth and sympathy, found its sentimentality complacent, banal and patronizing. The endless homilies, along the lines of 'The country's suddenly got tired and it's up to us ordinary people to keep things steady' were particularly hard to take.

The family was headed by Robert Newton and Celia Johnson. Mills played the nice young sailor who lived next door and who was finally reunited with their rebellious daughter (Kay Walsh) who had ideas above her station and ran off with a married man.

And there is John Mills playing a variation on his performance in In Which We Serve, *a variation still as solid and right as the original.*

Dilys Powell *Sunday Times*

ABOVE John Mills and Eileen Erskine in *This Happy Breed*.

Waterloo Road • 1945
A film directed by Sidney Gilliatt

Waterloo Road, an unpretentious cockney drama, was not just another wartime love story about a decent Tommy going absent without leave to stop his wife from jumping into bed with an unpleasant spiv, a smooth pin-table racketeer in a flashy suit. The film was also a bit of post-war propaganda to remind the cinema-going public that the British working classes were a bit of all right and knew the difference between right and wrong.

It was left to Alistair Sim, in his role of kindly doctor and narrator, to deliver the social message straight into the camera. This was just after John Mills (in his clearly defined role of representative of the people who had made sacrifices during the war) had given Stewart Granger (in his role of parasite) the bloody nose he so richly deserved.

Waterloo Road, that vivid and realistic study of London life, showed that John Mills, perhaps more than any other actor in British films, is able to portray the average young man-in-the-street on the screen. He has a real sympathetic quality, an authenticity which makes him down to earth, ordinary and likeable.

Peter Noble *Stage and Screen*

John Mills is also interesting to watch. British films ought to boost him. He has a tough but sympathetic style you don't often find in this movie Blunderland.

Ernest Betts *Daily Express*

If Waterloo Road *were not so English it would be French, which sounds like nonsense, but is really a deep thought.*

Helen Fletcher *Time and Tide*

BELOW Joy Shelton, Stewart Granger and John Mills in *Waterloo Road.*

Duet for Two Hands • 1945
A play by Mary Hayley Bell, directed by Anthony Pelissier and John Mills at Lyric Theatre.

A young poet in 1904, having had both his hands amputated, acquired a new pair, grafted from a corpse on to his living stumps. The hands once belonged to a murderer.

Duet for Two Hands, set in a lonely Gothic house in the Orkneys, provided West End audiences with a popular mixture of whimsy and Grand Guignol. Mills played the poet.

No critic has ever accused Mr Mills of slovenly utterance. He has one of the most beautiful voices on the stage and he uses it so that his seeming whispers can be heard at the back of the gallery.
Anthony Cookman *Tatler and Bystander*

The Way to the Stars • 1945
A film directed by Anthony Asquith
US title: Johnny in the Cloud

The Way to the Stars, made with the co-operation of the RAF and the USAAF, remains a deeply affecting tribute to Anglo-American relations during the war. Terence Rattigan's screenplay, a nostalgic mixture of courage and humour, quiet camaraderie and silent grief, is a classic example of British understatement.

Interestingly, not a single shot was fired in the film. All scenes of battle took place off-screen. The film relied entirely on character and atmosphere, limiting itself to two settings: the camp and the hotel in the local town where the men relaxed when they were off-duty. The acting, realistic yet sentimental, but never mawkish, was excellent throughout.

Mills played a young pilot, who was shattered by the death of a brother officer and felt he had no right to be getting married and having kids when he was courting death daily. He spoke John Pudney's poem, 'Johnny in the Cloud', specially written for the film, quite unselfconsciously, almost throwing it away and thereby, of course, making it even more moving. The scene he shared with Rosamund John, when he had to tell her that her husband had been killed, was faultless in its economy and reticence. The performance was and still is a model of its kind.

LEFT John Mills in *Duet for Two Hands*.

ABOVE John Mills and Rosamund John in *The Way to the Stars*.

Great Expectations • 1946
A film directed by David Lean

David Lean's *Great Expectations* remains one of the great Dickens films, memorable for its atmospheric opening scenes on the marshes and Pip's electrifying first meeting with the convict, Magwitch.

Pip, in any adaptation, is liable to end up playing a supporting role to the supporting actors and in this particular production the competition was formidable. There were definitive performances by Martita Hunt as Miss Havisham, Francis L. Sullivan as Jaggers, Bernard Miles as Joe Gargery, Alec Guinness as Herbert Pocket, Jean Simmons as the young Estella and O. B. Clarence as Wemmick's Aged P.

Mills's job was to hold the film together, which he did laudably. Strictly speaking, he was too old and it was difficult to reconcile him with Anthony Wager who played his younger self; the man seemed so much more common and coarse than the boy. The character and the story had been simplified. The ingratitude and snobbery were still there, but they were underplayed to such an extent that Pip emerged far more sympathetically than he does in the novel.

Lean's most original touch was to send Estella back to Satis House to live, like Miss Havisham, in dust and decay. (The re-creation of Miss Havisham's rooms was one of the many highlights of the film.) It was left to Pip to open the shutters and let the daylight in, a happy ending totally false to the novel, though one which Dickens's more sentimental readers had always wanted. However, even they could probably have done without the running hand-in-hand into the distance.

John Mills proceeds to give a performance which for attractive, sensitive, fine-shaded acting has rarely been excelled in films. This part puts him right at the top of our male stars – I mean the stars who really are actors.

Stephen Watts *Sunday Express*

He makes of this first personal character such a full-blooded, gracious young man that Pip actually has more stature here than he has in the book.

Bosley Crowther *New York Times*

It is John Mills's best and most sensitive performance in films.

Richard Winnington *News Chronicle*

ABOVE Alec Guinness and John Mills in *Great Expectations*.

OPPOSITE Martita Hunt and John Mills in *Great Expectations*.

So Well Remembered • 1947
A film directed by Edward Dmytryk

So Well Remembered is a long-forgotten adaptation of a novel by James Hilton about an idealistic newspaper editor and his materialistic wife. It was the first film to be made under an Anglo-American affiliation. Bosley Crowther, critic of the *New York Times*, put its social sincerity on a par with *The Citadel* and *The Stars Look Down*. The British critics did not doubt its sincerity, but found the story slow-moving and tedious.

Mr John Mills gives the most solid performance of his career.
Scotsman

John Mills is original and experienced enough not to be misled by the clichés of the leading part and what life can be wrung out of this preposterous person he gives us.
C. A. Lejeune *Observer*

The October Man • 1947
A film directed by Roy Baker

Eric Ambler's genteel, seedy boarding-house thriller was unbelievable but quite atmospheric, thanks to the art decoration by Vetchinsky and the dramatic *film noir* lighting by Erwin Hillier. Mills, in the title role, was just out of hospital after a head injury and liable to have a relapse any minute and jump under any passing train whistling through the night. He was suspected of having murdered one of the house guests.

The acting of John Mills as Jim Ackland possesses the sincerity and intensity which makes him one of the most sympathetic of our artists to watch on the screen.
Tribune

Mr John Mills is always an actor whom it is a pleasure to watch. He is quiet and good-mannered, and, even when perplexed in the extreme, manages that neurotic perplexity shall not distress others.
The Times

Mr Mills has never to my knowledge given an indolent, a casual or an insignificant performance.
Dilys Powell *Sunday Times*

It puts him right in the forefront of British actors.
News of the World

ABOVE John Mills and Juliet Mills in *The October Man*.

OPPOSITE Trevor Howard and John Mills in *So Well Remembered*.

Scott of the Antarctic • 1948
A film directed by Charles Frend

*Had we lived I should have had a tale to tell of
the hardihood, endurance and courage of my
companions which would have stirred the hearts
of every Englishman.*

Robert Falcon Scott

The British Antarctic Expedition's fatal journey to
the South Pole was an ideal choice for the Royal
Command film. The photography by Jack Cardiff,
Osmond Borradaile and Geoffrey Unsworth was
superb and there was also an excellent
impressionistic score by William Walton.

The actors, who had been chosen because of their
likeness to the men they were portraying, acted with
dignity, but such reticence that audiences, like Scott
before them, could only guess what was going on in
their hearts. The screenplay, ever mindful of the
feelings of survivors and relatives, preferred to
concentrate on the journey rather than their
characters. There was, however, a limit to what
could be done with close-ups of iced faces and men
hauling sledges across glacier and plateau. The
end result was a sincere tribute to human fortitude,
terribly worthy, but finally a bit dull. Certainly,
not nearly enough was made of the bitter
disappointment of finally reaching the Pole only to
discover that Amundsen had been there first and left
a cheeky request, asking Scott to forward a letter to
the King of Norway telling him of his success.

*The acting is led by John Mills, as Scott, and no
actor we have is better able to suggest sustained
courage and the highest integrity.*

Alan Dent *Illustrated London News*

*John Mills's portrayal of Scott is the greatest thing
he has ever done.*

Sunday Dispatch

*The missing element – and I hate to repeat a word
that film producers do not like – is poetry. Tragedy,
nobility have evaded this film of good intention. We
must make do with gentlemanly courage and
gentlemanly pathos from characters who do not
really come alive.*

Richard Winnington *New Chronicle*

RIGHT James Robertson Justice and John Mills in *Scott of the
Antarctic.*

The History of Mr Polly • 1949
A film directed by Anthony Pelissier

The History of Mr Polly was H. G. Wells's favourite novel and the film, faithful to its atmosphere, characters and dialogue, was clearly a labour of love.

Mr Polly, a frustrated shopkeeper with an insatiable hunger for bright and delightful experiences, is married to a nagging wife and surrounded by people he does not like. At the age of thirty-seven he decides he has had enough and runs away to find happiness, deep in the countryside, at an inn by a river.

Mills underplayed Polly's least amiable weakness, his penchant for polysyllabic words, though fortunately the best of them had been preserved. 'I'm not one of your Herculaceous sort,' he said. 'Nothing very wonderful biceptially.' Mills was especially delightful at the guzzling funeral luncheon (beautifully directed, acted and edited) when he was laughing nervously and showing off to a group of elderly female admirers who remembered the days when they had dandled him on their knees. 'My dandling days are over,' he announced. 'My turn to dandle.'

Finlay Currie's mad, drunken Uncle Jim was a comic version of his Magwitch and his first meeting with Polly paid homage to David Lean's *Great Expectations* and Pip's memorable first meeting with the convict on the marshes. The scenes which followed for possession of Potwell Inn and the triumphant watery eviction of Uncle Jim were excellent farce.

Despite the casting of Edie Martin as the old lady on the roof (and Edie Martin was the little old lady of all little old ladies in British films), the fire, the novel's great comic set piece, failed to be funny because the all-important dialogue was drowned by the deafening music on the soundtrack.

John Mills physically and in humour and sentiment is the ideal Polly and the part is ideal for him. It is a warmly human and lovely performance.
A. E. Wilson, *Star*

This Mr Polly is a flat undeveloping character who finally gives up all pretence of being anybody but our old John Mills.
Richard Winnington *News Chronicle*

ABOVE John Mills in *The History of Mr Polly*.

The Rocking Horse Winner • 1949
A film directed by Anthony Pelissier

The Rocking Horse Winner, on the printed page, is a fairy story: a brief, cruel fantasy about a stony-hearted mother and her sensitive, unloved son who has a gift for spotting winners while riding his rocking horse. Obsessed by his parents' need for more and more money, the boy rides himself to death.

The British censor did not care for D. H. Lawrence's cynicism and insisted a moral coda should be added: the mother must repent, the rocking horse must be burnt and the money must be used for benevolent purposes. The coda was totally unconvincing.

The boy was played by John Howard Davies who had created Oliver in the David Lean classic, *Oliver Twist*. Valerie Hobson played his mother and Mills had the small role of the chauffeur, the lame ex-batman, who fired the boy's imagination.

John Mills brings to the role of the handyman his special gifts of sincerity and simple kindness.
Daily Telegraph

BELOW John Mills and John Howard Davies in *The Rocking Horse Winner*.

The
Fifties

OPPOSITE John Mills in *Above Us the Waves*, 1955.

Morning Departure • 1950
A film directed by Roy Baker
US title: *Operation Disaster*

A submarine, on peacetime Asdic exercises, strikes
a stray, electronically controlled mine and sinks
fifteen fathoms deep. Out of a crew of sixty-five,
twelve men survive and wait to be salvaged. Eight
are able to make their escape; the remaining four are
left to die.

A real-life submarine disaster occurred just before
Morning Departure was due to open and there was
much heart-searching by both the film company and
the censor as to whether it should be released so
soon after the tragedy. In the end it was decided to
show it as a tribute to the Royal Navy and the
British naval tradition.

The film had a moving story to tell and told it
economically, without false heroics, in sober
documentary fashion, firmly resisting all box-office
temptations to compromise and provide a happy
ending. The action was totally gripping, the pace
throughout perfectly judged and the acting
beautifully restrained. The scene in which the men
drew cards to see who would have to stay behind
was particularly effective.

Mills's sympathetic and unassuming
performance, as the skipper, was impeccable,
notable for its quiet authority, moral integrity and
dignity.

*As the commanding officer of the submarine John
Mills gives one of his subtly understated
performances which have made his reputation.*
> Dilys Powell *Sunday Times*

*Mr John Mills, as you may imagine, plays the part
of the Lieutenant-Commander with such perfect
mastery that it is impossible to regard him as an
actor. He quite simply is a Lieutenant-Commander –
a truly magnificent performance.*
> Virginia Graham *Spectator*

RIGHT James Hayter, Michael Brennan, Richard Attenborough,
Nigel Patrick, Victor Madden, Andrew Crawford, George Cole
and John Mills in *Morning Departure*.

Top of the Ladder • 1950
A play by Tyrone Guthrie, directed by Tyrone Guthrie at St James's Theatre.

Guthrie's expressionistic play, a banal kaleidoscope in the German manner with Freudian additions, was a notable failure. The failure was due in part (as the author was the first to admit) to his decision to direct his play and not to cut obvious passages and repetitions.

Mills, playing a business tycoon on his death-bed, re-enacted key moments in his life from the age of five to fifty-five. The role was as long as Hamlet and Mills was never off the stage. He had to do his quick costume changes behind a screen, while he was still talking. His performance, constantly switching from elderly father to young man, and often in mid-movement while crossing the stage, was undoubtedly a *tour de force*, but it was not enough to save the play.

It would have been a dreary evening indeed but for Mr Mills who should never again be allowed to disappear into the film studios. He has a fine voice and can use it, and a sufficiently grand manner to tower above men taller than himself.
> Time and Tide

Here is a performance which is astonishing in its versatility as well as its technical brilliance.
> Manchester Guardian

Figure of Fun • 1951
A play by André Roussin, directed by Peter Ashmore at Aldwych Theatre.

It was not until the second act that the audience discovered that Mills was playing an English actor and what they had just been watching was the French comedy in which he was appearing.

In the first act, Mills was in his stage role of an artist whose girlfriend had just walked out on him. In the second act, he was the actor in his home who discovered his wife had just left him. In the third act, he was back on stage and so completely sozzled that the curtain had to be brought down on his performance.

The farce was very funny and Mills was so good in the serious moments that many people, who had seen André Roussin's play in Paris, regretted that the long monologue, in which he imagined he was accused of murdering his wife, had been cut.

John Mills, playing what amounts to John Mills playing John Mills, understandably fails to differentiate very clearly between the two parts. However, keying up his charm and puckering up his face, he sprints through a taxing marathon with enormous zest and mobility.
> Kenneth Tynan *Evening Standard*

LEFT John Mills and Rachel Kempson in *Top of the Ladder*.
OPPOSITE Peter Bull and John Mills in *Figure of Fun*.

Mr Denning Drives North • 1951
A film directed by Anthony Kimmins

Mr Denning, a wealthy aircraft manufacturer, accidentally killed his daughter's lover, an Argentinian criminal. The screenplay, having begun in heavy melodrama with music to match, then drifted into farce when he lost the body. ('I've been kicking myself ever since', he told his wife, played by Phyllis Calvert.) The audience, uncertain which lane Mr Denning was meant to be driving in – either the tragic or the comic lane – was confused and laughed in all the wrong places, only to find that the film was meant to be funny after all.

Mr Mills is an excellent actor and the scenes in which he shows us the anguish of a man with a dead body on his mind are very moving.

Roy Nash *Star*

The Gentle Gunman • 1952
A film directed by Basil Dearden

The Gentle Gunman, a mixture of thriller and classroom debate on the Anglo-Irish question, was based on Roger MacDougall's play and its stage origins showed. Mills was the gunman, a member of the IRA, who had recognized the futility of violence and rejected terrorism. He was branded a traitor by his mates and sentenced to death. He was saved at the very last minute by the appearance of the very men he was said to have betrayed. There they were, roaring drunk, driving down the road, pursued by the constabulary and a hail of bullets. It was an extraordinary denouement, more appropriate to a Keystone Cop film.

Mr Mills, it is true, sounds as if he came from Dorset, and looks so patently good that it is difficult to believe he ever nurtured enmity against anyone.

Spectator

LEFT Phyllis Calvert and John Mills in *Mr Denning Drives North.*

ABOVE Dirk Bogarde, Joseph Tomelty and John Mills in *The Gentle Gunman.*

75

The Long Memory • 1953
A film directed by Robert Hamer

Mills played a man who had been framed for a murder he had not committed. He came out of prison, having served a twelve-year sentence, determined to exact revenge. The marshes of the Thames Estuary, with its mudflats and rotting barges in and around Gravesend, provided an excellent atmospheric location, but Hamer's efforts to turn second-rate material into an English *Quai des Brumes*, with Mills in the Jean Gabin role, did not really come off.

Mr Mills, given the right sort of part, is one of the most convincing and most heart-stirring players of the British screen.

Manchester Guardian

Mr John Mills we all know to be an accomplished actor, but his playing here, monotonously sullen, fails to express the corroding bitterness which would explain the man and the plot.

Dilys Powell *Sunday Times*

John Mills energetically sustains the angry mien of a Rover whose faith in the whole Boy Scout movement has been strangled out of existence.

Fred Majdalany *Daily Mail*

RIGHT John Mills in *The Long Memory*.

76

The Uninvited Guest • 1953
A play by Mary Hayley Bell, directed by Frank Hauser at St James's Theatre.

The Uninvited Guest, a mixture of melodrama and social document, concerned a young lad who had been incarcerated in a mental asylum and kept there by his mother for twenty years. Mills, brimming with resentment, looked and behaved (according to W. A. Darlington, critic of the *Daily Telegraph*) as if he were the fruit of a union between Uriah Heep and Miss Murdstone. The little dead smile was particularly chilling; but it was his vermilion wig, a symbol of the fiery temper which had ruined his life, which stole most of the notices.

As Candy, the unwanted son of Lady Lannion, John Mills wears a bright red wig, gives a characteristically straight-faced performance, and comes nowhere near the tragic heights that his wife, Miss Bell, presumably had in mind for her leading character.

Ian Hamilton *Spectator*

Mr Mills himself gave a very fine performance, taut, menacing, immensely pitiful.

Harold Hobson *Sunday Times*

Charley's Aunt • 1954
A play by Brandon Thomas, directed by John Gielgud at New Theatre.

John Gielgud directed the famous farce as if it were a high comedy by Oscar Wilde, but Brandon Thomas has not got Wilde's wit and needs much rougher treatment.

Mills, in the traditional black satin, fichu, wig and cap, happily blowing smoke rings with the aid of a cigar, looked like a cross between Queen Victoria and a chimpanzee. His funniest moments included pouring tea and milk into poor old Spettigue's topper and emptying the entire salad bowl on to his plate. His performance was highly agile and great fun.

Mr John Mills is unflagging in spirits and unfailing in comic resource; there is never any danger of a wobble while he is on the stage.

T. C. Worsley *New Statesman and Nation*

Mr Mills's Babberley glitters with a cheerful, healthy, athletic fin de siècle *decadence; this Babberley has a dandified purity, he is Wilde in innocence.*

Harold Hobson *Sunday Times*

ABOVE John Mills and Joan Greenwood in *The Uninvited Guest*.
OPPOSITE John Mills and Philip Stainton in *Charley's Aunt*.

78

Hobson's Choice • 1954
A film directed by David Lean

Harold Brighouse's classic Lancashire comedy is a fine and enduring example of the Manchester school of sentimental realism. Mills was excellent as Willie Mossop, the master bootmaker who suddenly found himself engaged to Maggie, Mr Hobson's elder and bossy daughter, an old maid at thirty. 'You're going to marry me,' she told him. 'I'd really rather marry Ada, Maggie, if it's all the same with you,' he replied.

The performance was notable for its warmth and affection for the role and the play. The troubled-looking face and the pudding-basin haircut were just right. Walking down the cobbled street, Mills's matchstick figure, in its tight-fitting suit, looked as if it had just stepped out of a painting by J. S. Lowry. (The play is set in Salford, Lowry's home town.) Mossop's development from meekness to tentative assertiveness was both comic and touching.

Brenda de Banzie was an equally memorable Maggie, but Charles Laughton, regrettably, was allowed to turn Hobson into an overextended, self-indulgent music hall 'drunk' act, which was given a jaunty, boozy musical accompaniment on the soundtrack. The performance, coarse and vulgar, inevitably, was more farcical than tyrannical.

This is great comedy acting – laughable, loveable, pathetic – with every detail of dress, make-up and demeanour superbly right.
Fred Majdalany *Daily Mail*

As for John Mills as the boot-hand, it is a joy to see this actor in a role which extends his uncommon gifts of sensibility and comedy.
Dilys Powell *Sunday Times*

RIGHT Brenda de Banzie, Charles Laughton and John Mills in *Hobson's Choice*.

The Colditz Story • 1955
A film directed by Guy Hamilton

Colditz Castle in Saxony, in World War II, housed officers of the allied nations who had succeeded in escaping from other German POW camps. It was said to be impregnable and escape-proof.

'Welcome to Colditz. I'm sorry I couldn't meet you at the station,' said one inmate to the new arrival (John Mills), adopting a cheerful, laid-back tone which was to be symptomatic of the whole film's approach. The privations and hardships of POW life were ignored. War was a jolly adventure, played by public school chaps. There was no attempt at characterization. The British, French, Dutch and Poles spoke in their mother tongues and conformed to national stereotypes. The German guards were caricatured for easy laughs.

The script concentrated on the escapes in a straightforward and superficial manner with some humour but no tension. Every incident was based on fact and some were spectacular. A French officer, for instance, cheekily somersaulted over the wire fence, a feat the stuntmen had the greatest difficulty in emulating. Mills was cast as the enthusiastic officer in charge of British escapes. He walked out of Colditz disguised as a German officer.

The film was shown with great success at the Portland Borstal Institution. The very next day two boys absconded.

OPPOSITE Lionel Jeffries, Bryan Forbes and John Mills in *The Colditz Story*.

BELOW Anton Diffring, Theodore Bikel and John Mills in *The Colditz Story*.

The End of the Affair • 1955
A film directed by Edward Dmytryk

The End of the Affair was based on the Graham Greene novel in which a wife, finding her lover dead, promised God that if He would bring him back to life, she would give him up for ever. Her prayer was answered and she kept her promise. The wife and lover were played by Deborah Kerr and Van Johnson.

Mills, as the comically earnest private detective in a raincoat and bowler, provided an entertaining interlude and was much nearer to the Graham Greene original than many people thought.

John Mills contributes a charming comi-pathetic study, out of context, belonging to some other film, but nice.

Virginia Graham *Spectator*

The film was not a good film, and at moments it was acutely painful to see situations that had been so real to be twisted into stock clichés of the screen.

Graham Greene

ABOVE Van Johnson and John Mills in *The End of the Affair*.

84

Above Us the Waves • 1955
A film directed by Ralph Thomas

Above Us the Waves was the story of the attacks made on the German battleship, *Tirpitz*, by midget submarines and British human torpedoes. The film, the latest in a very long line of such celebrations of British reserve and laconic humour, dealt as usual in types rather than characters and, inevitably, had nothing to say about World War II which had not been said countless times before. Mills was cast in his familiar role of dependable skipper.

John Mills gives what is rapidly becoming a hackneyed performance, and most of the players get little chance to display more than routine competence.

Derek Hill, *Films and Filming*

BELOW John Mills, Lee Patterson, William Russell, Anthony Wager, James Kenny, Donald Sinden, Harry Towb and Michael Medwin in *Above Us the Waves.*

Escapade • 1955
A film directed by Philip Leacock

A sixteen-year-old schoolboy organized a stunt to advocate the cause of peace. He stole a plane and flew off to the Four Powers in Vienna. His message was simplistic: 'We do not wish to kill children of any other school. Men cannot always see the truth of a simple proposition. Perhaps it is for the children to lead the way.'

Sadly, neither the boy nor the flight were seen in the film and his message had to be read out by another pupil back home. Roger MacDougall's *Escapade* remained a photographed play, slackly directed and quite unconvincing. Mills was cast as the boy's father, a professional militant pacifist. It was a role which required him to be belligerent, self-centred and self-dramatizing. Yvonne Mitchell played his wife and Alistair Sim played the headmaster.

BELOW Yvonne Mitchell, John Mills and Alistair Sim in *Escapade*.

OPPOSITE Jeremy Spenser and John Mills in *It's Great to be Young*.

It's Great to be Young • 1956
A film directed by Cyril Frankel

It's Great to be Young described a mutiny by the pupils of a co-ed. grammar school when a popular teacher (John Mills) was sacked by the headmaster (Cecil Parker). If the film had been made in Hollywood, it would have starred Mickey Rooney and Judy Garland and had big production numbers by Busby Berkeley. Made in England in the 1950s, its aims were more modest and its one and only number, deliberately amateurish, was just the sort of thing you would expect from children still at school and whose slang was as defunct as *Greyfriars* itself.

Mills was totally convincing in his role of born teacher and good sport who put the school orchestra above everything. It was easy to believe he could inspire devotion and loyalty in his pupils. His likeable performance had plenty of energy and there was some nifty work at the piano, too.

It's Great to be Young proved so popular with Singaporean children that the education authorities were reported as having deeply regretted allowing it into the country.

Mr Mills is always at his best fighting lost causes, in uniform and out, and this new film is the most enjoyable thing he has done for some time.

Jympson Harman *Evening News*

The Baby and the Battleship • 1956
A film directed by Jay Lewis

The Baby and the Battleship, a slender but jolly farce, cast John Mills, Richard Attenborough and Bryan Forbes as three tars who were left holding a baby when the baby was smuggled aboard during NATO manoeuvres in the Mediterranean. They hid him in lockers, lifeboats, bathrooms, punishment cells and even, on one occasion, an oven. Mills was the dimwitted one and watching him, trying to wrack what little brain he had, was very amusing. The Neapolitan baby was adorable and got rave reviews.

War and Peace • 1956
A film directed by King Vidor and Mario Soldati

The cast included Audrey Hepburn as Natasha, Henry Fonda as Pierre, Mel Ferrer as Andrei and Oscar Homolka as Field Marshal Kutuzov. Mills, a very cockney Russian, played Platton, the philosophic peasant, who was taken prisoner by the French and accompanied Pierre on the long retreat from Moscow. He was shot by the wayside and died with a smile on his face and a dog in his lap.

This version of Tolstoy's novel was totally eclipsed some ten years later by Sergei Bondarchuk's Russian film with its magnificently staged battle scenes and visually stunning romantic images of death and glory out of Eugène Delacroix.

Around the World in 80 Days • 1956
A film directed by Michael Anderson

Audiences did not come to see the Jules Verne classic to find out whether Phileas Fogg would win his bet but to see how many stars they could spot in Mike Todd's 4-million-dollar spectacular. They had to be quick; some roles were so small, the actors barely had time to register. Forty-four stars appeared in cameo roles, among them Noël Coward, Marlene Dietrich, John Gielgud, Buster Keaton, Frank Sinatra, Fernadel, Beatrice Lillie, Robert Morley, George Raft and Red Skelton. Mills played a coughing London cab-driver, one of the last people to delay Fogg.

The film's most stylish moment was when Fogg (David Niven) was flying over the Alps in a balloon and Passepartout (Cantinflas) leant out of the basket to scoop up some snow for the champagne bucket.

ABOVE David Niven, John Mills and Cantinflas in *Around the World in 80 Days*.

OPPOSITE ABOVE Martyn Garrett, John Mills and Bryan Forbes in *The Baby and the Battleship*.

OPPOSITE BELOW Henry Fonda and John Mills in *War and Peace*.

Town on Trial • 1957
A film directed by John Guillermin

There were some critics who rated *Town on Trial* as one of the finest British thrillers in years, admiring its acting, atmosphere and crisp narrative drive; but there were also those who were not so convinced by the advisability of fashioning an English crime story on a Hollywood model. The Home Counties took on a decidedly phoney American look and feel.

Mills was cast as a tough and unorthodox detective trying to find out who was strangling girls with nylon stockings near a country club. The class-conscious town, outraged by his strong-arm tactics, tried to get him taken off the case. The film's climax had the detective and the murderer together on the roof of the church.

We lack the climate of violence to commit the perfect screen crime.

Philip Oakes *Evening Standard*

John Mills is most persuasive as the police-investigator when he is not bullying his suspects in a way which we don't like to think of as English at all, and which, anyhow, does not suit Mr Mills in the least.

Alan Dent *Illustrated London News*

John Mills is superb as a conscientious detective.
Harris Deans *Sunday Dispatch*

LEFT Alec McCowen and John Mills in *Town on Trial*.

91

The Vicious Circle • 1957
A film directed by Gerald Thomas
US title: *The Circle*

Mills played an eminent Harley Street specialist who was suspected of being involved in the murder of an actress. He is seen here being questioned by a detective-inspector.

John Mills as the doctor is only required to look harassed – which may well come naturally to him in a wardrobe which would horrify Harley Street.
Monthly Film Bulletin

I Was Monty's Double • 1958
A film directed by John Guillermin
US title: *Hell, Heaven, or Hoboken*

I Was Monty's Double was an account of one of World War II's cheekiest and most audacious bluffs, a monumental D-day hoax. In order to divert attention away from Europe, Monty went on an inspection tour of North Africa in 1944 – only it was not Monty at all but an obscure Pay Corps officer impersonating him.

Clifton E. James was engaged to re-create his wartime role. It was a part he had originally accepted with the greatest reluctance, feeling he lacked the self-confidence to sustain it. His vulnerability was oddly touching. However, his likeness to Monty was so uncanny that audiences had no difficulty in believing that he had hoodwinked everybody.

Mills, characteristically brisk, Cecil Parker, characteristically bumbling, were cast as the two officers in intelligence who masterminded the whole affair.

It was a pity that the producers felt it necessary to add an absurd fictional climax in which Monty was kidnapped by a German commando group and then rescued by a two-man operation with one machine-gun between them. Neither Mills nor Bryan Forbes could make this schoolboy nonsense credible.

ABOVE John Mills and Roland Culver in *The Vicious Circle*.

OPPOSITE Clifton E. James and John Mills in *I Was Monty's Double*.

Dunkirk • 1958
A film directed by Leslie Norman

Dunkirk itself was a great defeat and a great miracle. *Dunkirk*, the film, was a great disappointment. The production was conscientious and sincere, but lacking in the passion and anger which had informed such masterpieces about World War I as *All Quiet on the Western Front* and *Paths of Glory*. The cheap patriotic music which accompanied the little boats as they sailed down the Thames was a typical misjudgement.

The inherent weakness in the script was to try to tell the story of the evacuation of the British Expeditionary Forces, a mass exercise, through just three individuals: an embittered journalist (Bernard Lee), a garage owner (Richard Attenborough) and a reluctant corporal (John Mills). The corporal was forced to take command of his squad when it was separated from its unit and the officer was killed. The whole sequence could have come out of any war film of the period.

Dunkirk was at its best on the beaches: the bullets ripping up the sand; the hurried prayers ('Oh, Mother of Mercy, keep me through this'); the soldiers queuing patiently in the water being picked off by enemy aircraft; the interrupted church service. But even here the film was not sufficiently epic. There were simply not enough men and there certainly were not enough boats.

John Mills gives another convincing performance as the corporal.
Campbell Dixon Daily Telegraph

I have nothing against Mr Mills except that he has campaigned through so many films on sea and land that his honest, worried features take the bite out of any danger to which he might be exposed.
William Whitebait New Statesman and Nation

Our Finest Hour is in danger of becoming A Cracking Bore.
Derek Granger Financial Times

RIGHT Sean Barrett, Bernard Lee and John Mills in *Dunkirk*.

94

Ice Cold in Alex • 1958
A film directed by J. Lee Thompson
US title: *Desert Attack*

Ice Cold in Alex described a 600-mile journey across the Libyan desert from Tobruk to Alexandria in an ambulance in 1942. Despite German patrols, minefields, a snow storm, leaking radiators and a German spy, there was not that much tension. A key scene, for instance, in which the ambulance gradually edged its way up a sandy slope and failed to reach the top, was not improved by the unsubtle music on the soundtrack. The actual framing of individual shots was poor, leaving the actors too often just standing in a line. The one genuine bit of excitement was when the spy (Anthony Quayle) became trapped in quicksand. The scene was a straight crib from *La Salaire de la Peur* (*Wages of Fear*) and none the less gripping second time round.

Mills was cast as a very blond, pooped-out officer, living on his frayed nerves. With Quayle and Harry Andrews constantly by his side, he looked like a David among Goliaths. He had a much-publicized scene with Sylvia Syms (as a nurse), which was strictly superfluous and made even more superfluous when the censor insisted Miss Syms buttoned up her shirt.

The title referred to the glass of lager Mills had promised himself when he reached Alexandria. When the film was shown in America, its running time was cut to sixty-four minutes and it looked to Eugene Archer, a critic of the *New York Times*, as if the movie were 'an advertisement for shaving cream and draught beer'. Thirty years later, the final scene at the bar in Alex was actually used in an advertisement.

Ice Cold in Alex won the International Critics Award at the Berlin Film Festival.

BELOW Harry Andrews, Anthony Quayle and John Mills in *Ice Cold in Alex*.

Tiger Bay • 1959
A film directed by J. Lee Thompson

Tiger Bay, a gripping little thriller, efficiently directed with plenty of pace, was enormously popular, and rightly so. The success was due in no small measure to twelve-year-old Hayley Mills's unforgettable screen debut as a naughty tomboy, a snub-nosed liar, who witnessed a murder and befriended the murderer, a gentle and handsome Polish seaman played by Horst Buchholz.

Mills had the less sympathetic role of the superintendent who questioned her. The scenes they shared undoubtedly gained an extra piquancy from the audience knowing that in real life the actors were father and daughter.

Buchholz was so charming and his relationship with the girl so touching that many cinemagoers would have been quite happy for the murdered woman's lover to have been arrested and hanged in his place.

Tiger Bay had more than a superficial resemblance to the 1951 *Hunted* (starring Dirk Bogarde and six-year-old Jon Whiteley); and the resemblance would certainly have been remarked on more had the leading role been played, as had been originally intended, by a boy actor.

Little Miss Mills acts her father off the screen.
Harold Conway *Daily Sketch* headline

But if you hear it said that she acts her father off the screen, take a second look. In one of his best, most off-beat performances, Mills gives his daughter every possible opportunity to steal every scene they have together. It is to their joint credit that she gets away with bare-faced robbery each time.
Derek Monsey *Sunday Express*

ABOVE Hayley Mills and John Mills in *Tiger Bay*.

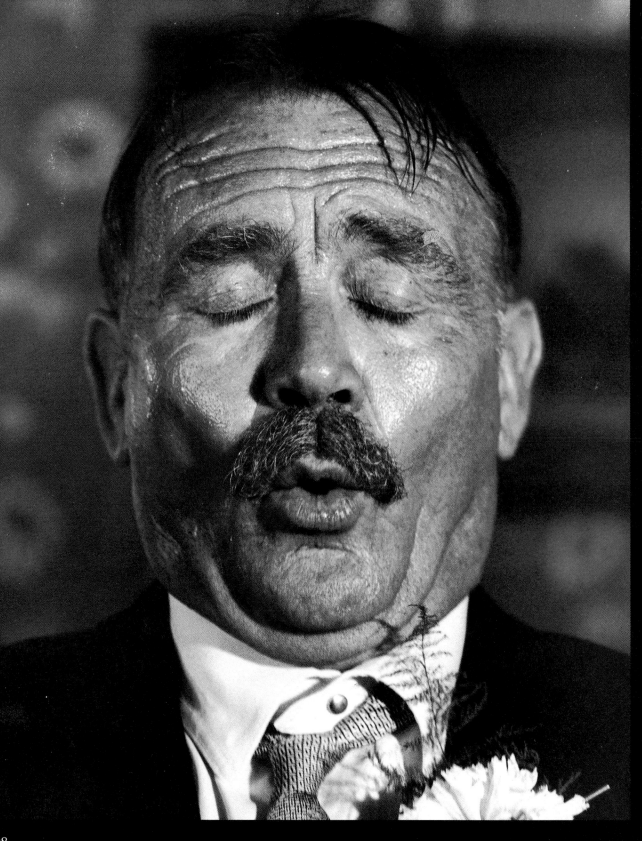

The
Sixties

Summer of the Seventeenth Doll • 1960

A film directed by Leslie Norman
US title: *Season of Passion*

Ray Lawler's rowdy, bawdy, over-rated drama was about two canecutters from Queensland who, for the last sixteen years, had been coming down to Sydney during their lay-off period to spend five months with a couple of barmaids. Mills was the canecutter who discovered that his barmaid had got married and he had been provided with a prudish substitute.

The play had scored a big success on the London stage, not least because it was Australian. The film was a disappointment. Although it had been shot on its home ground, it did not feel that Australian, largely because British and American actors were cast in the leading roles.

John Mills, crew-cut, cocky, jerking like a stringed puppet, is splendid.

Derek Monsey *Sunday Express*

The Swiss Family Robinson • 1960

A film directed by Ken Annakin

Walt Disney's version of the well-known children's classic was filmed on location in Tobago with lots of imported animals and provided simple, wholesome entertainment for the whole family. There was a funny fight with the pirates in which everybody got blown up and nobody got hurt. There was also an amusing point-to-point race with the Robinson family riding on a donkey, an elephant, a zebra and an ostrich, and all going off in different directions.

OPPOSITE Anne Baxter, Ernest Borgnine, Angela Lansbury and John Mills in *Summer of the Seventeenth Doll*.

ABOVE Kevin Corcoran, John Mills, Tommy Kirk, Dorothy McGuire and James MacArthur in *The Swiss Family Robinson*.

Tunes of Glory • 1960
A film directed by Ronald Neame

Tunes of Glory, a story of military honour in a wintry Scottish barracks in peacetime, described a highly theatrical clash between the new battalion commander and the old commander, ending in the death of both men.

Mills was the new broom, Basil Barrow, a product of Eton, Oxford, Sandhurst and Whitehall, a strict disciplinarian. He was dismissed as 'a spry wee gent' and 'toy soldier' by the old guard, the coarse, hard-drinking ex-ranker, Jock Sinclair (Alec Guinness), who constantly undermined his authority.

Barrow had survived a Japanese POW camp and the horrors he had experienced there were always inherent in Mills's performance, though never openly stated. There was a spectacular loss of temper at a cocktail party, which prepared the ground for the final mental breakdown and suicide.

Mills, in one of his finest performances, and Guinness, in one of his finest performances, complemented each other perfectly. (It is interesting to note that the two actors agreed to swap roles just before filming began.) What was so good about James Kennaway's screenplay was the way the audience's sympathies shifted from the fiery-headed, popular braggart to the nerve-racked, repressed martinet and back again.

Mills charted Barrow's inner torment, loneliness and increasing isolation most movingly and went on to win the prize for best actor at the Venice Film Festival.

OPPOSITE Allan Cuthbertson, Alec Guinness and John Mills in *Tunes of Glory*.

BELOW Duncan Macrae, John Mills, Alec Guinness and Gordon Jackson in *Tunes of Glory*.

The Singer Not the Song • 1961
A film directed by Roy Baker

Is it the song which is good or merely the singer which makes it so?

The film described a battle between a good priest and a bad bandit in a remote Mexican village. John Mills was the priest and Dirk Bogarde was the bandit who hated the Catholic Church and was convinced the song was worthless.

Mills's big scene came when a seventeen-year-old girl asked the priest to kiss her. She wanted a 'real kiss, a love-kiss, the sort of kiss that can be a sin because I shall know all my life that you loved me so much that you would even sin for me'. And the priest, who did indeed love her, kissed her, watched by the smirking bandit. 'I'm the soul of discretion,' he said. 'Forget I'm here.'

What the priest did not know, and never found out, was that the bandit was also harbouring a hopeless passion for him. The final shoot-out ended with both men locked in mortal embrace and the bandit pretending to say an act of contrition just to please the priest.

Mills was clearly not happy. Certainly he was not acting in the same film as Bogarde's villain. When he had accepted his role, he had been led to believe that Marlon Brando was going to play the bandit.

LEFT Dirk Bogarde and John Mills in *The Singer Not the Song.*

105

Ross • 1961

A play by Terence Rattigan, directed by Glen Byam Shaw at Eugene O'Neill Theatre, New York (transferred to Hudson Theatre).

Terence Rattigan's play traces the events which led T. E. Lawrence, that legendary and charismatic figure of the Middle East, to seek anonymity in the ranks of the RAF as Aircraftsman Ross. The role had been created by Alec Guinness in London. Glen Byam Shaw totally rethought his production for New York. The playing was much more physical. Mills's Lawrence was a man of action.

Mills is magnificent, deeply moving.
Robert Coleman New York Mirror

John Mills brings to the title role the intellectual arrogance and flip behaviour that makes his spiritual destruction the more poignant and compelling.
John McClain New York Journal-American

Mr Mills's portrayal of the all-important central role is nothing short of superb . . . He is a stunning actor who deserves far greater recognition.
Richard Watts Jr. New York Post

OPPOSITE John Mills in *Ross*.

Flame in the Streets • 1962

A film directed by Roy Baker

John Mills was cast as a staunch trade-unionist, passionately fighting ignorance and racial prejudice on the factory floor, who found he was not so resolutely liberal when it came to his own daughter (Sylvia Syms) marrying a Jamaican schoolteacher (Johnny Seka).

Flame in the Streets, based on Ted Willis's well-meaning, if laboured stage play, *Hot Summer Night*, suffered from being released while memories of such powerful working-class dramas as *The Angry Silence* and *Saturday Night, Sunday Morning* were still fresh in cinemagoers' memories.

Mills, always persuasive as a man of principle, his heart in the right place, fought his corner convincingly and was suitably appalled by his wife's racism; but Brenda de Banzie, too middle-class and behaving as if she had married beneath her, was miscast.

John Mills, always happier as a cockney spark rather than as a gent, gives Jacko the thrust of an amiable noisy terrier.
James Breen Observer

BELOW Johnny Seka and John Mills in *Flame in the Streets*.

Tiara Tahiti • 1962
A film directed by William T. Kotcheff

A colonel, a former clerk in civilian life, deeply conscious of his social inferiority, was constantly undermined by a captain, the son of his former boss, who treated him with insufferable public school condescension. When the opportunity arose the colonel had him cashiered. Years later, after the war, the captain had his revenge.

James Mason was the captain, an idle, immoral, dissolute waster-turned-beachcomber, who was determined to thwart the colonel's plans to build a hotel on the island of Tahiti. Swanning around with characteristic charm, Mason was amusingly patronizing: 'Honestly, I've always liked you!' He was the British class system in action.

Mills, as the pompous upstart with a pseudo-Sandhurst accent, had two comic monologues, neatly enhanced by the uncertainty of his vowels. He also had a fine moment of seriousness when he complained bitterly that no matter what he achieved in life, he would always be to Mason and his kind 'your little clerk'.

Tiara Tahiti, which began promisingly enough, looked as if it was going to be *Tunes of Glory* all over again, but this time played for comedy. Unfortunately, the screenplay, unsure of its mood and style, did not have the courage of its cruel convictions and failed to use the island setting either for local colour or witty comment.

The Valiant • 1962
A film directed by Roy Baker
Italian title: *L'Affondamento della 'Valiant'*

The *Valiant* was a battleship lying in Alexandria Harbour in 1941. Two Italian frogmen were captured after they had laid a mine under her. The British captain (John Mills) tried to find out where they had fitted the mine and when it was going to go off. In the battle of wits which followed, the Italians refused to divulge any information and the captain was driven into acts of inhumanity, such as denying a wounded prisoner hospital treatment. Despite the exaggerated ticking of a clock, there was not that much tension.

The Valiant *is one of those tight-lipped exercises which are almost unimaginable without the presence of John Mills in the cast.*

> Felix Barker *Evening News*

Captain Mills's stiff-upper-lip does not so much as quiver.

> Thomas Wiseman *Sunday Express*

Power of Persuasion • 1963
A play by Gert Hofmann, directed by Anthony Quayle and John Mills at Garrick Theatre.

Power of Persuasion was an allegory on Nazism. Mills played a government clerk in a small German town. He was the archetypal puny little man in a baggy suit and bowler hat, sporting a toothbrush moustache. The man may have looked humble and servile on the outside, but thirty years of unrewarded drudgery had left him seething with resentment and greed. There was a terrifying moment when, inflamed by drink and a lust for power, he mounted the table and harangued the world – a little Hitler in the making.

As the nervous, bent, embittered clerk slowly achieving power and self-respect through the adrenaline of violence and hate, John Mills gives a terrifying study of the dehumanising nature of envy and greed.

> Milton Shulman *Evening Standard*

ABOVE John Mills in *Tiara Tahiti*.

OPPOSITE ABOVE Roberto Risso, Robert Shaw and John Mills in *The Valiant*.

OPPOSITE BELOW Anthony Quayle and John Mills in *Power of Persuasion*.

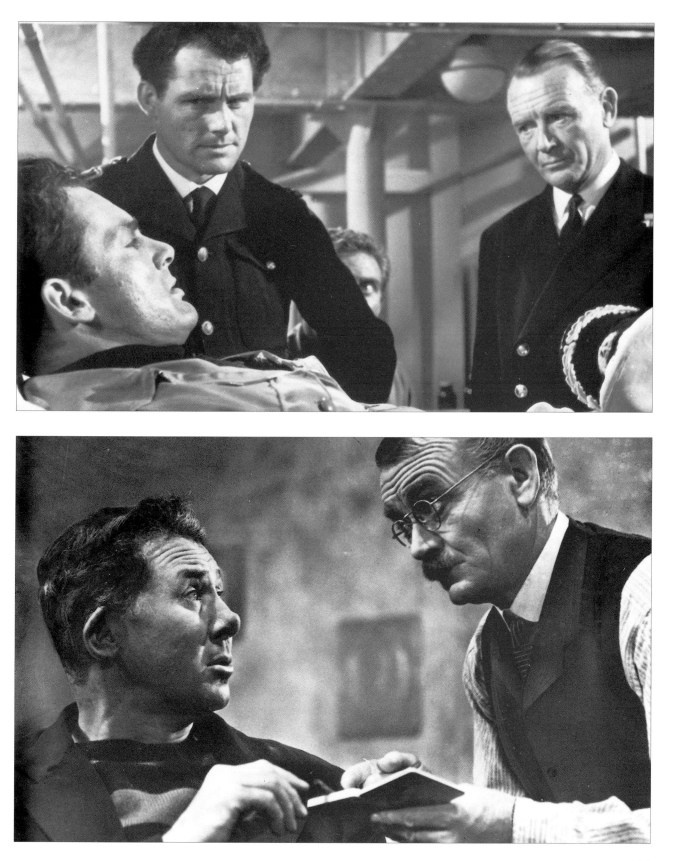

The Chalk Garden • 1964
A film directed by Ronald Neame

Despite having jettisoned most of Enid Bagnold's flowery artifice, *The Chalk Garden* still made an uncomfortable transition from stage to screen. In the theatre, the play had concentrated on the grandmother and governess, brilliantly acted by Edith Evans and Peggy Ashcroft. In the cinema, the emphasis shifted to the granddaughter, a much less interesting character. Mills played the butler.

John Mills does his decent, dogged and quizzical best.

Philip Oakes *Sunday Telegraph*

BELOW Hayley Mills, John Mills and Felix Aylmer in *The Chalk Garden*.

OPPOSITE John Mills in *The Truth About Spring*.

The Truth About Spring • 1965
A film directed by Richard Thorpe
Television title: *The Pirates of Spring Cove*

The Truth About Spring, set aboard a scruffy fishing boat in the Caribbean, starred Hayley Mills in her first romantic role. It was all so wholesome it hurt. The pace was funereal and the humour heavy-handed. Mills was cast as her rascally old father, a genial beachcomber in search of treasure and managing to outwit all the crooks on the islands.

Ponderously coy comedy romance with John Mills rather surprisingly winning the cuteness stakes in a flurry of winks and eyebrow-raising as the grizzled, whimsical, old salt.

Monthly Film Bulletin

John Mills sports a beard more luxuriant than that of Father Goose.

Robin Bean *Films and Filming*

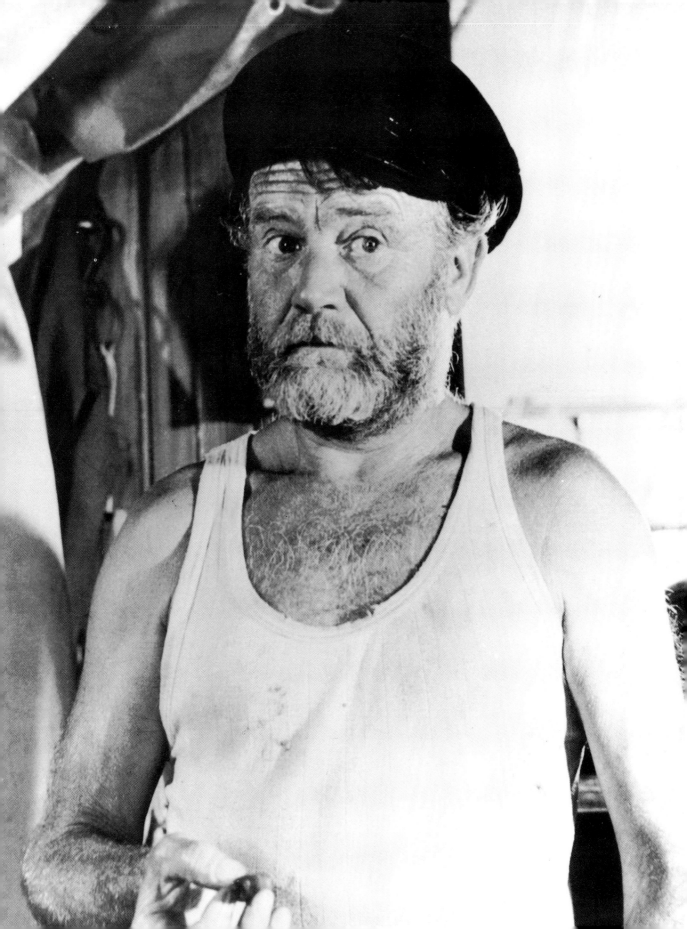

King Rat • 1965
A film directed by Bryan Forbes

King Rat, a much-underrated movie, deserves to be far better known. It was different from most POW films in that it was not a story of escape but a story of survival. Set in the Changhi Gaol on the island of Singapore in 1945, the script concentrated on the physical and moral degradation of the prisoners.

The rat of the title was Corporal King (well played by George Segal), who ran the camp's black market, ruthlessly exploiting every human weakness. Everybody was on his payroll from the colonel downwards. The men were just as much his prisoners as they were of the Japanese.

Mills had the small but important role of the colonel who tried to bribe the Provost Marshal (Tom Courtenay) with a commission in order to get him to drop charges against the camp's catering officer who had been fiddling the rations. The scene, excellently played by both actors, was particularly interesting because it was so ambivalent. It was never clear whether the colonel wanted him to drop charges in order to maintain discipline or whether he, too, was conniving with Corporal King and wanted to save his own skin.

ABOVE Tom Courtenay and John Mills in *King Rat*.

112

Operation Crossbow • 1965
A film directed by Michael Anderson
US title: *The Great Spy Mission*

Operation Crossbow was World War II as an all-star schoolboy adventure: a lamentable mixture of fact and the wildest melodrama, which purported to describe the attempts to locate and destroy Germany's V2 rockets at source. The preposterous climax, in which the underground factory was blown up, was space fiction out of *The Guns of Navarone*. The special effects department also blew up a few houses in an unconvincing attempt to simulate the London blitz. It would have been better to have used some genuine newsreel footage.

The cast included George Peppard, Tom Courtenay, Sophia Loren, Lilli Palmer and Anthony Quayle. Mills made a brief appearance as a pillar of military intelligence.

Everybody but Lassie seems to be in the film.
The Times

BELOW John Fraser, Trevor Howard, John Mills and Richard Todd in *Operation Crossbow*.

113

The Wrong Box • 1966
A film directed by Bryan Forbes

Two ancient brothers, who lived in adjoining mansions and had not seen each other in forty years, stood to inherit a fortune, but only at the expense of the other's life. They were the last surviving members of a tontine. A tontine is a financial arrangement by which subscribers to a common fund each receive an annuity during their lifetime, which increases as their number is diminished by death, until the last survivor enjoys the whole income.

The elder brother determined to murder the younger. A bewhiskered, night-shirted Mills had a hilarious sequence when he rose from his sick-bed and, grabbing anything that came to hand – poison, poker, cord, paperweight, penknife – still somehow failed to kill him. Finally, beside himself, spluttering with rage, he called him a pedantic, boring old poop and hurled a vase of flowers after him. 'Too late to apologize,' said the brother, played by Ralph Richardson, who was indeed wonderfully, manically boring.

The fault with *The Wrong Box*, based on a story by Robert Louis Stevenson, was that it had too many comedians in too many cameo parts not being very funny. Even Mills and Richardson, who were, presumably, in the leading roles, ended up playing cameo parts.

BELOW John Mills and Michael Caine in *The Wrong Box*.

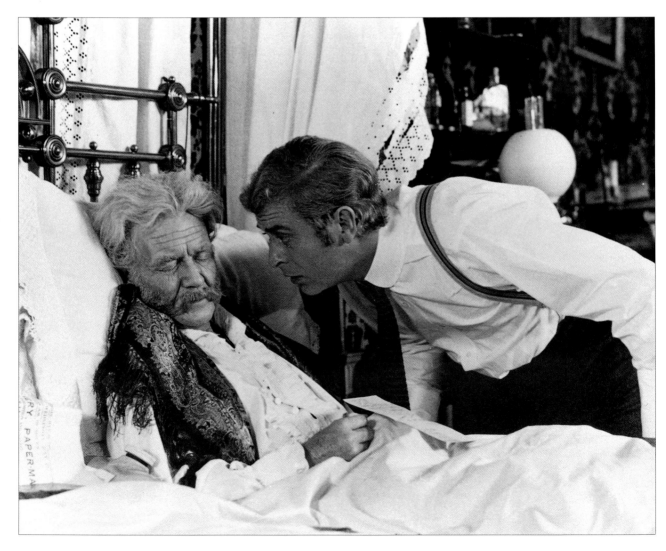

The Family Way • 1967
A film directed by Roy Boulting

The Family Way, based on Bill Naughton's play, *All in Good Time*, was about a young husband who was unable to consummate his marriage with his parents sleeping in the next room. His wife was philosophical: 'I don't care if it never happens. What you never have you don't miss.' His father was outraged: 'What a disgrace! Just suppose it leaked out at the gasworks. I'd never live it down.'

In his peak-cap, Mills looked like a sparrow under a rain-tub. He might have stepped out of a play by either Harold Brighouse or Stanley Houghton. The film, which did not hide its stage origins, could have done with a little less pretty technicolour and a bit more of the Bolton grit Mills brought to his role.

There was an excellent scene when the father deliberately picked on his son ('I can still lick the young uns!') and challenged him to an elbow match, which, when his son saw how terrified his dad was of losing, he let him win.

The reconciliation at the end gained an additional poignancy because the audience knew that Mills was not the boy's father. The boy had been fathered by his best mate, whom he had taken with him on his honeymoon!

John Mills as a beery old dad with a straggly moustache, and shirt without collar, gives one of the best performances of his life. It's a wonderful portrait of a working man.

Ian Christie *Daily Express*

John Mills has been playing working-class types for over twenty years, never, to my mind, convincingly, because, intelligent and observant though he is, a middle-class sensitivity is ineradicable from his character.

Raymond Durgnat *Films and Filming*

ABOVE Barry Foster, John Mills, Marjorie Rhodes, Hywel Bennett, Liz Fraser and Wilfred Pickles in *The Family Way*.

115

Chuka • 1967
A film directed by Gordon Douglas

Mills played an ex-Bengal lancer who had been cashiered from the British army for drunkenness. He was now in charge of a band of dishonoured and disgraced American officers in an isolated and beleaguered prairie fort, waiting for the Red Indians to attack. Impeccably dressed for battle, Mills came out of his command post and was immediately transfixed by an arrow before he even had time to find out whether he was still a coward or not. *Chuka* was one of those very rare occasions when the US cavalry failed to arrive at the last minute and the whole fort was slaughtered.

Chuka was a solitary gunfighter and he was played by Rod Taylor.

John Mills shooting it out in Cowboy and Indian country is a phenomenon not to be missed.
Cecil Wilson *Daily Mail*

John Mills is the colonel; his sadism accords ill with those twinkling eyes and that old familiar and utterly dependable furrowed brow.
Peter Davalle *Films and Filming*

The theme of disillusionment and the nursing of shattered ideals obviously appeals to him, and when the script is right the result is devastatingly good.
Clive Hirshhorn *Sunday Express*

Lady Hamilton – Zwischen Smach und Liebe • 1969
A film directed by Christian Jaque
English title: *Emma Hamilton*

The film was hysterical rather than historical. Certainly there were very few people who could take Emma's affairs with Lord Nelson and the Queen of Naples seriously. Mills played Emma's husband, Sir William Hamilton.

Run Wild, Run Free • 1969
A film directed by Richard C. Sarafian

A lonely bachelor befriended a young mute, a problem child, who *wouldn't* speak. He introduced the lad to the flora and fauna of Dartmoor and taught him to train a kestrel and ride. The boy was finally shocked into speech when a wild pony was trapped in a peat bog. It would have been difficult not to have been moved by young Mark Lester pleading with the pony not to die.

Mills, as the bachelor, acted with kindly, tweedy unobtrusiveness.

A great deal too is due to that brand of warm humanity which John Mills brings to so many parts.
Felix Barker *Evening News*

OPPOSITE John Mills and Rod Taylor in *Chuka*.

ABOVE John Mills and Michele Mercier in *Lady Hamilton*.

RIGHT John Mills and Mark Lester in *Run Wild, Run Free*.

Oh! What a Lovely War • 1969
A film directed by Richard Attenborough

The film version of this famous satire on the terrible carnage of World War I seems much better now than it did in 1969, when it invited comparison with Joan Littlewood's original stage production. As memories of Littlewood's brilliant production recede, so the film's stature grows.

Field Marshal Haig is cast as the villain: a self-centred, homicidal idiot, always planning 'one more final offensive', regardless of loss. He is confident the British will win in the end because they have more men to lose than the Germans. He puts himself in the hands of God ('I feel every step I take is guided by the Divine Will') and prays for victory before the Americans come.

Haig is first seen selling tickets at the turnstile of a pier, admitting the public to the 'ever-popular war game – battles, songs and a few jokes'. Later he is discovered singing, dancing and leap-frogging over another staff officer's back. His office is at the top of a helter-skelter.

The impressive thing about Mills's performance was that, despite the highly stylized context of the film, he himself resisted all attempts to caricature. His portrait of an orthodox and deeply unimaginative professional soldier, was frighteningly real.

The final shot of the film haunts the memory still: the camera tracked back to reveal a countryside full of neatly laid-out crosses stretching, so it seemed, into infinity.

RIGHT John Mills in *Oh! What a Lovely War.*

The Seventies

OPPOSITE John Mills in *Dulcima*, 1971.

Ryan's Daughter • 1970
A film directed by David Lean

Ryan's Daughter was an intimate love story, four years in the making and costing (reported to be $4,000,000). Robert Bolt's screenplay, a mixture of Thomas Hardy and D. H. Lawrence, was set in Ireland during the Troubles of 1916 and described a love affair between a schoolmaster's wife (Sarah Miles) and a British Officer (Chris Jones), who had been invalided out of the front line and was still suffering from shell-shock. Robert Mitchum played the schoolmaster.

The film, much maligned, was chiefly memorable for its storm sequences during which the villagers dredged up boxes of arms out of the sea. The magnificent coastline was superbly photographed by Freddie Young. The *mise-en-scène* was breathtaking.

Mills, totally unrecognizable, was cast as the crippled and dumb village idiot, who was also in love with the schoolmaster's wife. Before shooting began, Mills spent many hours watching films showing patients with brain damage, observing how they walked, their posture and angle of head. He gave an unforgettable performance. It was quite unlike anything he had done before and deservedly won him an Oscar.

A masterpiece by John Mills.
> Richard Barkley *Sunday Express*

John Mills is merely superb.
> Judith Crist *New York Magazine*

John Mills gives a perfect performance.
> Henry Hart *National Board of Review*

He is brilliantly effective, with an eloquence words could not improve.
> Charles Champlin *Los Angeles Times*

This is the kind of acting that gets people Academy Awards, because the acting is so conspicuous.
> Pauline Keel *New Yorker*

LEFT John Mills in *Ryan's Daughter*.

Adam's Woman • 1970
A film directed by Philip Leacock

Adam's Woman was a love story set in Australia in the 1840s during her penal colony days. Mills played the Governor of New South Wales, Sir Philip McDonald, who tried to improve prison conditions.

Young Winston • 1971
A film directed by Richard Attenborough

Carl Foreman's screenplay was based on Winston Churchill's *My Early Life* and gave an epic account of Winston's medal-hunting, publicity-seeking adventures as war correspondent and soldier on the North-West Frontier, in the Sudan and South Africa, where his escape from the Boers made him a world celebrity.

Simon Ward played Winston. Mills made a guest appearance as General Sir Herbert Kitchener, who is seen here leading his troops against 60,000 dervishes in the Battle of Omdurman.

ABOVE Beau Bridges, Jane Morrow and John Mills in *Adam's Woman*.

RIGHT John Mills in *Young Winston*.

124

Dulcima • 1971
A film directed by Frank Nesbitt

Dulcima was based on H. E. Bates's rural novella about a miserly, dirty and drunken Gloucestershire farmer who was infatuated with a bosomy country girl at least thirty years his junior. When she fell in love with a well-spoken, dreamily romantic gamekeeper, the farmer shot him dead. The story suffered from neither relationship being believable; nor did the two young actors have the weight to carry the abrupt and melodramatic climax which was straight out of a Victorian novel.

Mills, unexpectedly cast as an absurdly randy old man, whose money was hidden all over the house (under carpets, in old newspapers and biscuit tins), had one moment of rage which was real and frightening. 'Open the door, you bitch!' he screamed. 'I'll take a stick to you, you lying bitch!' But, for the most part, he was too comic a figure, almost Chaplinesque when he wriggled out of his trousers and got into bed still wearing his shirt, hat and smoking a cigarette. His most interesting scenes were those at the market where he showed himself to be a fly dealer.

What *Dulcima* really needed was a French treatment by Marcel Pagnol and a director like Claude Berri of *Jean de Florette* fame.

Mills, perhaps rather too determined not to let his officer-class antecedents show through, at times edges a skilful cameo into caricature.
                          Derek Malcolm *Guardian*

John Mills is over-intent on gaining our sympathy for the rustic Parker and does not develop the grotesque side of his nature.
                  Margaret Tarratt *Films and Filming*

Lady Caroline Lamb • 1972
A film directed by Robert Bolt

John Mills played Lord Canning who advised Lord Melbourne (Jon Finch) to concentrate on his political career and ditch Lady Caroline Lamb (Sarah Miles). The cast also included Laurence Olivier as Wellington, Ralph Richardson as George IV and Richard Chamberlain as Byron.

OPPOSITE John Mills and Carol White in *Dulcima*.

BELOW Jon Finch, Sarah Miles and John Mills in *Lady Caroline Lamb*.

Veterans • 1972

A play by Charles Wood, directed by Ronald Eyre at Royal Court Theatre.

When the play was touring the regions, audiences were deeply offended by the bad language. 'Don't use that word again in front of my wife!' said one irate man during a performance at the Theatre Royal, Brighton.

Veterans, a satire on films and filming, had come out of Charles Wood's experiences during the making of *The Charge of the Light Brigade* in Turkey and was an affectionate in-joke at the expense of John Gielgud who had played Lord Raglan.

Mills had the more serious role of a veteran of countless British war films and famous for 'doing marvellous oil-smeared things in the water'. The likeness to Mills ended there. The actor was much given to indecent exposure and the play opened with his flashing himself to the ambassador's daughter.

The question, as to whether he would be thrown off the set and what would happen to his career, was frankly far less interesting than listening to Gielgud, in his role, gossiping away, dropping bricks all over the place.

The final scene had the two men discussing whether or not to appear in the West End in a dreadful new play. 'They'll love it, if we do it,' said the Gielgud character. The audience tittered nervously, uncertain if this were another in-joke, this time at the expense of Charles Wood himself.

ABOVE John Gielgud and John Mills in *Veterans*.

At the End of the Day • 1973

A play by William Douglas Home, directed by Robert Chetwyn at Savoy Theatre.

At the End of the Day had its roots in an over-confident, pipe-smoking Labour Prime Minister (John Mills) calling a premature general election, resulting in a landslide victory for the Conservatives. William Douglas Home's somewhat patronizing comedy allowed audiences to have easy laughs at two well-known public figures. The jokes were, on the whole, better than the seriousness which tended to drag.

Michael Denison, who was cast as the Conservative Prime Minister (plummy voice, grand piano and all), did not come on until the last act and then proceeded to walk off with the play. The closing moments were particularly funny when he inadvertently picked up the Labour leader's acceptance speech and read it out to the assembled television cameras under the impression that it was his own speech.

John Mills's forte as an actor is sincerity and suffering heroically under fire. He clings eagerly to a few moments of seriousness, but it needed a comedian to exploit the discomfiture of a man inflated by arrogance.

Frank Marcus *Sunday Telegraph*

BELOW Michael Denison and John Mills in *At the End of the Day*.

129

Oklahoma Crude • 1973
A film directed by Stanley Kramer

Here was a drama as crude as the oil itself, especially in that memorable moment when the hobo hero (George C. Scott) urinated down the leg of the villain, while holding a rifle to his throat.

Faye Dunaway's role was a man-hating wildcat who ran an oil rig. Mills was cast as her ne'er-do-well father who had deserted her before she was born and now wanted to make it up to her. He hired the hobo to protect her from the murderous clutches of a giant oil company.

Mills's spry and engaging performance was likened to Micawber, Kipps and Charles Ruggles, but the part failed to live up to its initial promise, petering out long before he fell to his death from a derrick, shot by Jack Palance's exemplary villain, a cigar-chomping vulture in a bowler hat.

The English voice of John Mills is as out of place in this Oklahoma oilfield as the sound of a lute would be at a brass band concert.

Ian Christie *Daily Express*

BELOW George C. Scott, John Mills and Faye Dunaway in *Oklahoma Crude*.

The Good Companions • 1974
A musical by Johnny Mercer, Ronald Harwood and André Previn, directed by Braham Murray at Her Majesty's Theatre.

J. B. Priestley's novel about a touring concert party and the three people who rescue it from bankruptcy had already been staged in 1931. It now returned to the same theatre as a musical with Judi Dench as Miss Trant, Christopher Gable as Inigo Jollifant and John Mills as Jess Oakroyd, the old carpenter.

John Mills as Jess Oakroyd conveys the steadfast worth of character which makes him one of the ornaments of the British stage, and he has a song and dance called 'Ta, Luv' in which he is absolutely show-stopping.

Harold Hobson *Sunday Times*

John Mills, as a gnarled little Yorkshire man in a cloth cap, gets to do a tap-dance to a reception that could easily seem a little fulsome if he had actually risen from the dead.

Kenneth Hurren *Spectator*

OPPOSITE Judi Dench and John Mills in *The Good Companions*.

130

Separate Tables • 1977
A play by Terence Rattigan, directed by Michael Blakemore at Apollo Theatre.

Terence Rattigan's double bill offered its two leading actors two wildly different roles within the same setting of a Bournemouth hotel. The supporting cast played the permanent guests and staff.

In *Table Number One* (originally called *Table by the Window*) Mills was a former Labour politician, now turned journalist, who had once been married to a top fashion model he had tried to murder. In *Table Number Two* he was a bogus major arrested for an assault on a woman in a cinema.

Table Number One always had been the weaker of the two plays and had dated badly. The verbal and physical violence was so mechanical as to be merely melodramatic. *Table Number Two*, a thinly disguised homosexual play based on a much publicized court case of a famous person in the early 1950s, was infinitely more rewarding.

The major was a timid, shy, lonely man, frightened of women, pathetically hiding behind a pseudo-public school accent and a military moustache. Mills's beautifully understated performance made many people regret that he had never acted the failed schoolmaster in Rattigan's *The Browning Version*.

ABOVE Jill Bennett and John Mills in *Separate Tables*.

132

The Devil's Advocate • 1977
A film directed by Guy Green

Morris West's best-selling novel was about a Vatican priest who was sent into the wilds of Abruzzi to investigate the claims to sainthood of an obscure Italian peasant who had been shot by partisans during World War II. The priest, dying of cancer, gradually became aware of his lack of faith. Mills's performance was notable for its gentleness and compassion.

The Thirty-Nine Steps • 1978
A film directed by Don Sharp

This version, the third remake of John Buchan's spy yarn, was at its most exciting in the long opening sequence which led to the murder of Mills, in his role of British intelligence officer, stabbed to death at St Pancras Station. The film failed to maintain the pace and excitement once the story shifted to Scotland. There were so many cross-references to the 1936 Alfred Hitchcock classic that homage became plagiarism. Robert Powell was cast as Hannay, a role previously played by Robert Donat and Kenneth More.

ABOVE LEFT John Mills in *The Devil's Advocate*.

ABOVE RIGHT John Mills in *The Thirty-Nine Steps*.

Zulu Dawn • 1979
A film directed by Douglas Hickox

Zulu Dawn, a prequel to the infinitely superior *Zulu*, told the story of the Battle of Isanshlwana in 1879 in which the British were massacred. The script was clearly on the side of the Zulu warriors and voiced all the correct anti-imperialist, anti-war sentiments, while at the same time indulging the cinema-going public's love of a good slaughter. There was very little to the film but the killing of people in large numbers. Mills played the High Commissioner, Sir Bartle Frere.

Quatermass • 1979
A serial by Nigel Kneale, directed by Piers Haggard for Thames Television.

The story was set in the future when law and order had broken down. Mills was cast as Quatermass, the brilliant scientist, who came out of retirement to save the world.

ABOVE John Mills in *Quatermass*.

OPPOSITE Burt Lancaster and Simon Ward in the back row and John Mills and Peter O'Toole in the front row in *Zulu Dawn*.

The Eighties

OPPOSITE John Mills in *A Tale of Two Cities*, 1989.

Galloping Foxley • 1980
Directed by Claude Whatham for Anglia Television.

Galloping Foxley was one of Roald Dahl's *Tales of the Unexpected*. A quiet and respectable solicitor was outraged to find his regular railway seat occupied by a bearded stranger. Rattled, he became more and more convinced that the man was the sadistic head boy who had flogged him half a century earlier.

The story brought back vivid memories to Mills of the mental and physical torture he had suffered during his first term at school in Norwich. There he had been stripped and beaten with a heavy hairbrush and then shut up in a cupboard with an acetylene lamp which had asphyxiated him with its fumes. He had also been in danger of being blown up at any minute.

Young at Heart • 1982
Directed by Stuart Allen for ATV.

Young at Heart, a television sitcom, provided a light-hearted look at the problems of retirement. John Mills and Megs Jenkins, reunited thirty-three years after *The History of Mr Polly*, were so popular that they went on to make another two series.

LEFT John Mills in *Galloping Foxley*.

BELOW Megs Jenkins and John Mills in *Young at Heart*.

Goodbye Mr Chips • 1982

A musical by Roland Starke and Leslie Bricusse, directed by Patrick Garland at Chichester Festival Theatre.

There is very little in James Hilton's novel to turn into a musical; although those who had seen the pre-war movie remembered that Robert Donat and Greer Garson had spent an inordinate amount of time waltzing in Vienna for no good reason.

The Chichester production was based on the 1969 musical film, starring Peter O'Toole and Petula Clark, which had, somewhat strangely, updated the action. The maudlin and flimsy story-line was wisely put back to its correct period, the show leaning very heavily on the audience's sentimentality and patriotism.

Mills, in his role of bumbling, much-loved schoolmaster (Greek scholar turned soft-shoe-shuffle man), sang the tinkly pathos with conversational ease.

Sir John Mills, gentleman as he is, perfectly captures in his performance Chips' decency and the other old British virtues of the period that gave birth to him, but his lines do not allow him to show him in depth.

Anthony Masters *The Times*

Sir John Mills at the age of 74 takes on Mr Chips, a role which requires him to age almost 40 years in one evening, sing and dance. He does so with endearing gallantry and charm; his voice rides over the music in a sort of speech way.

Nicholas de Jongh *Guardian*

Little Lies • 1983

A play by George Caruso, directed by Tony Tanner at Wyndham's Theatre.

It was never clear why theatregoers were being offered an ill-constructed and unfunny adaptation of Arthur Wing Pinero's *The Magistrate* when the genuine article was readily available and soon to be revived with great success at the National Theatre.

Mills, just once, on entering his office after a night on the tiles, totally dishevelled, his trousers filthy dirty, did look like Mr Posket, the magistrate fallen from grace. He made much of the agony of putting a pair of spectacles on his bruised nose and even more of spewing his tea all over an old army acquaintance.

LEFT John Mills in *Goodbye Mr Chips*.

OPPOSITE John Mills in *Little Lies*.

The Petition • 1986
A play by Brian Clark, directed by Peter Hall at the National Theatre (transferred to Wyndham's Theatre).

A retired Tory general, reading *The Times* one morning, was shocked to find that his wife (Rosemary Harris) had signed a petition to ban the bomb and intended to speak at a rally.

Mills, the quintessential Englishman, was perfect casting for the reactionary eighty-year-old general, a blinkered, pompous, patronizing gent, married to the army, whose happiest years had been spent fighting in World War II. He paced the carpet as he might pace a parade ground.

There was a particularly moving moment - as fine as anything he had done on stage and screen - when, learning his wife had at the most three months to live, he broke down, sobbing uncontrollably. His performance took many critics by surprise.

John Bury's fissured set gave the play a bit of class. Taking his cue from the wife's remark to the effect that they had lived their lives on different planets, Bury provided two separate rooms, reflecting their individual characters, yet so designed as to make one acting area.

But the revelation to me was John Mills who I have always thought of as a rather circumspect actor.

Michael Billington *Guardian*

He is very moving. I did not think he had it in him, and I eat my hat.

Michael Ratcliffe *Observer*

Who's That Girl? • 1987
A film directed by James Foley

Who's That Girl? was a disastrous remake of the classic screwball comedy, *Bringing Up Baby*. Mills played an eccentric millionaire who owned half of New York.

OPPOSITE Rosemary Harris and John Mills in *The Petition*.

BELOW Madonna and John Mills in *Who's That Girl?*

Pygmalion • 1987
A play by George Bernard Shaw, directed by Val May at Yvonne Arnaud Theatre (transferred to Plymouth Theatre, New York).

Mills played Alfred Doolittle, the thinking dustman, one of the undeserving poor, who came into a fortune and found himself, much against his will, a gentleman and trapped by middle-class morality. Peter O'Toole was cast as Henry Higgins, the brilliant professor of phonetics, who transformed Doolittle's daughter, a cockney flower girl, into a lady.

John Mills, an outstanding actor, endows Alfred Doolittle with the manner of a real person instead of the improbable clown to whom audiences have grown accustomed. The result is that this Doolittle rises to the level of the great comic creations of Shakespeare and Molière.
William B. Collins *Philadelphia Inquirer*

Spit MacPhee • 1988
A mini-series directed by Marcus Cole for Australian Television.

The series was based on James Aldridge's Australian novel about an orphan's battle to determine his own future. Mills appeared in the first episode as the boy's crazy old grandfather who set fire to their ramshackle home.

A Tale of Two Cities • 1989
Directed by Philippe Mounier for Granada Television.

Mills played Jarvis Lorry, the kindly banker and friend to the Manettes, in this Anglo-French production which unexpectedly, but quite rightly, put Charles Darnay rather than Sydney Carton firmly at the centre of Charles Dickens's story. The crowd scenes, acted by a handful of extras, were particularly unconvincing.

ABOVE John Mills in *Pygmalion*.

OPPOSITE Philip Hancock and John Mills in *Spit MacPhee*.

LEFT John Mills in *A Tale of Two Cities*.

Ending Up • 1990
Directed by Peter Sasdy for Thames Television.

Kingsley Amis's cruel novella, on the senility of the aged, was described as black comedy but it was, in fact, much nearer to tragedy. The story was too uncomfortable for laughs and it was not surprising that Thames Television delayed showing it until after Christmas. It was hardly a play to be watching with elderly relatives over the festive season.

Mills had the least sympathetic role of the cashiered officer who had just learned that he had but three months to live. The man was intolerable and deeply offensive, tormenting everybody with his malicious jokes and sarcastic snubs; even his Christmas presents managed to be horrid.

Some critics thought Mills's essential decency showed through; they must have missed the glowering hatred when his choicest rudeness was accepted as a joke.

Harnessing Peacocks • 1993
Directed by James Cellan Jones for ITV.

The heroine of Mary Wesley's novel was a part-time gourmet cook for wealthy old ladies and an expensive part-time mistress for wealthy men – her peacocks. John Mills played Bernard, the art dealer, an old rake who had spent his wild youth seducing scores of women, including the ones the heroine now cooked for.

ABOVE John Mills and Peter Davison in *Harnessing Peacocks*.

LEFT John Mills, Wendy Hiller, Googie Withers and Lionel Jeffries in *Ending Up*.

147

Awards and Honours

1947   Picturegoer and Film Weekly Gold Medal
       Best Actor: *Great Expectations*

       National Film Award
       Best Actor

1948   National Film Award
       Best Actor

1950   National Film Award
       Best Actor

       Sketch Theatre Award
       For outstanding achievement in the theatre:
       Top of the Ladder

1951   National Film Award
       Best Actor

1960   CBE

       Venice Film Festival Award
       Best Actor: *Tunes of Glory*

1961   Films and Filming Award
       Best Actor

       Blue Ribbon Box Office Award (American)

1964   Blue Ribbon Box Office Award (American)

1965   Blue Ribbon Box Office Award (American)

1966   Blue Ribbon Box Office Award (American)

1967   The Film Daily Filmdom's Famous Five Poll (American)
       Best Actor: *The Family Way*

1968   San Sebastian Film Festival Award
       Best Actor: *The Family Way*

1971   Academy of Motion Pictures Arts and Sciences Award
       Best Supporting Actor: *Ryan's Daughter*

       Hollywood Foreign Press Association
       The Golden Globe Award
       Best Supporting Actor: *Ryan's Daughter*

       The Golden Rose Bowl Award*
       Best Supporting Actor: *Ryan's Daughter*

       Grand Order of Water Rats
       The Ambassador Award: awarded for the personality
       over the past year who did most to enhance Britain's
       international show biz status

1976   Knighthood

1979   Evening News British Film Award

1980   *Up in the Clouds, Gentlemen Please* published

1981   Variety Club of Great Britain
       Midland Region Award

       World Sporting Club
       Decanter in recognition of services to the British
       Film Industry

1982   British Academy of Film and Television Arts Award
       A Special Tribute

1988   Retrospective at the National Film Theatre to celebrate
       his eightieth birthday

* The Golden Rose Bowl Award is awarded on the voting of the public in New York and Los Angeles.

OPPOSITE John Mills in *Ryan's Daughter*, 1970.

Chronology

THEATRE

DATE	TITLE	WRITER	ROLE	DIRECTOR	THEATRE
1929 Mar.	The Five O'Clock Girl	Book: Guy Bolton and Fred Thompson	Chorus	John Harwood	London Hippodrome

1929/1930 *The Quaints. Tour of the Far East**

	TITLE	WRITER	ROLE	DIRECTOR	
	Journey's End	R. C. Sherriff	Lieutenant Raleigh	James Grant Anderson	
	Young Woodley	John Van Druten	Young Woodley	James Grant Anderson	
	Hamlet	William Shakespeare	Osric Second Player Second Gravedigger	James Grant Anderson	
	Mr Cinders	Book and Lyrics: Clifford Grey and Greatrex Newman Additional lyrics: Leo Robin Music: Vivian Ellis and Richard Meyers	Jim Lancaster	James Grant Anderson	
	When Knights Were Bold	Charles Marlowe		James Grant Anderson	
	Funny Face	Book: Fred Thompson and Paul Gerard Smith Lyrics: Ira Gershwin Music: George Gershwin	Dugsie Gibbs	James Grant Anderson	
	The Girl Friend	Adapted from Philip Bartholomae and Otto Harbach's *Kitty's Kisses* by R. P. Weston and Bert Lee Music and lyrics: Con Conrad, Gus Kahn, Richard Rodgers and Lorenz Hart	Jerry	James Grant Anderson	
	So This is Love	Book: Stanley Lupino and Arthur Rigby Music: Hall Brody Lyrics: Desmond Carter	Hap J. Hazzard	James Grant Anderson	

* The tour included: Calcutta, Rangoon, Penang, Ipoh, Kuala Lumpur, Serenbam, Malacca, Singapore, Colombo, Bombay, Madras, Hong Kong, Shanghai, Hangkow, Peking, Tientsin, Lahore, Quetta, Simla, Poona, Rawalpindi, Landi, Khotal and Karachi.

DATE	TITLE	WRITER	ROLE	DIRECTOR	THEATRE
1930 Dec.	Charley's Aunt	Brandon Thomas	Lord Fancourt Babberley	Amy Brandon Thomas	New
1931 Apr.	Cochrane's 1931 Revue	Noël Coward	Various	Frank Collins	London Pavilion
May	London Wall	John Van Druten	Birkinshaw	Auriol Lee	Duke of York's
Oct	Cavalcade	Noël Coward	Joe Marryot	Noël Coward	Drury Lane

DATE	TITLE	WRITER	ROLE	DIRECTOR	THEATRE
1932 Sept.	Words and Music	Noël Coward	Various	Noël Coward	Adelphi
1933 June	Give Me a Ring	Book: Guy Bolton, R. P. Weston and Bert Lee Lyrics: Graham John Music: Vivian Ellis	Jack Brookes	William Mollison	London Hippodrome
1934 Dec.	Jill Darling!	Book: Marriott Edgar and Desmond Carter Music: Vivian Ellis	Bobby Jones	William Mollison	Saville
1936 Mar.	Red Night	James Lansdale Hodson	Private Syd Summers	Miles Malleson	Queen's
May	Aren't Men Beasts?	Vernon Sylvaine	Roger Holly	Leslie Henson	Strand
1937 June	Floodlight	Beverley Nichols	Various	C. Denis Freeman	Saville
Dec.	Talk of the Devil	Anthony Pélissier	Roger Miller	Claud Gurney	Piccadilly
1938 May	Pélissier's Follies of 1938	Various	Various	Anthony Pélissier	Saville
Dec.	A Midsummer Night's Dream	William Shakespeare	Puck	Tyrone Guthrie	Old Vic
1939 Jan.	She Stoops to Conquer	Oliver Goldsmith	Young Marlow	Tyrone Guthrie assisted by Frank Napier	Old Vic
Mar.	We At The Crossroads	Keith Winter	Tommy	Murray Macdonald	Globe
Apr.	Of Mice and Men	John Steinbeck	George	Norman Marshall	Gate
May	Of Mice and Men	John Steinbeck	George	Norman Marshall	Apollo
1942 Sept.	Men in Shadow	Mary Hayley Bell	Lew	Bernard Miles and John Mills	Vaudeville
1945 June	Duet for Two Hands	Mary Hayley Bell	Stephen Cass	Anthony Pelissier and John Mills	Lyric
1947 June	Angel	Mary Hayley Bell		John Mills	Strand
1950	The Damascus Blade	Bridget Boland	Daniel Bonaught	Laurence Olivier	tour
Oct.	Top of the Ladder	Tyrone Guthrie	Bertie	Tyrone Guthrie	St James's
1951 Oct.	Figure of Fun	André Roussin adapted by Arthur Macrae	Freddie	Peter Ashmore	Aldwych
1953 May	The Uninvited Guest	Mary Hayley Bell	Candy	Frank Hauser	St James's
1954 Feb.	Charley's Aunt	Brandon Thomas	Lord Fancourt Babberley	John Gielgud	New

DATE	TITLE	WRITER	ROLE	DIRECTOR	THEATRE
1961 Dec.	Ross	Terence Rattigan	Ross	Glen Byam Shaw	Eugene O'Neill, New York
1962	Ross	Terence Rattigan	Ross	Glen Byam Shaw	Hudson, New York
1963 Sept.	Power of Persuasion	Gert Hofmann translated by Donald Watson	Otto Moll	Anthony Quayle and John Mills	Garrick
1972 Mar.	Veterans	Charles Wood	Laurence D'Orsay	Ronald Eyre	Royal Court
1973 Oct.	At the End of the Day	William Douglas Home	Henry Jackson	Robert Chetwyn	Savoy
1974 July	The Good Companions	Musical based on the novel by J. B. Priestley Book: Ronald Harwood Lyrics: Johnny Mercer Music: André Previn	Jess Oakroyd	Braham Murray	Her Majesty's
1975 Dec.	Great Expectations	Musical based on the novel by Charles Dickens Book by Hal Shaper and Trevor Preston Lyrics: Hal Shaper Music: Cyril Ornadel	Joe Gargery	Alan Lund	Yvonne Arnaud, Guildford transferred O'Keefe Centre, Toronto
1977 Jan.	Separate Tables	Terence Rattigan	Mr Malcolm Major Pollock	Michael Blakemore	Apollo
1982 Aug.	Goodbye Mr Chips	Musical based on the novel by James Hilton Book: Roland Starke Music and lyrics: Leslie Bricusse	Mr Chips	Patrick Garland and Christopher Selbie	Chichester
1983 July	Little Lies	Joseph George Caruso freely adapted from *The Magistrate* by Arthur Wing Pinero	Mr Posket	Tony Tanner	Wyndham's
1986 July	The Petition	Brian Clark	General Sir Edmund Milne	Peter Hall	National
	The Petition	Brian Clark	General Sir Edmund Milne	Peter Hall	Wyndham's
1987 Mar.	Pygmalion	George Bernard Shaw	Alfred Doolittle	Val May	Yvonne Arnaud, Guildford
	Pygmalion	George Bernard Shaw	Alfred Doolittle	Val May	Plymouth, New York
1991	An Evening with John Mills				Australian tour
1992	An Evening with John Mills				English tour

DATE	FILM	SCREENPLAY	ROLE	DIRECTOR
1932	The Midshipmaid (US title: *Midshipmaid Gob*)	Stafford Dickens based on play by Ian Hay and Stephen King-Hall	Midshipman Golightly	Albert de Courville
1933	Britannia of Billingsgate	C. H. Moresby-White and Ralph Stock based on play by Christine Jope-Slade and Sewell Stokes	Fred	Sinclair Hill
	The Ghost Camera	H. Fowler Mear based on story by J. Jafferson Farjeon	Ernest Elton	Bernard Vorhaus
1934	A Political Party	Syd Courtenay, Lola Harvey and Leslie Fuller	Tony Smithers	Norman Lee
	The River Wolves	Terence Egan based on play *The Lion and the Lamb* by Edward Dignon and Geoffrey Swaffer	Peter Farrell	George Pearson
	The Lash	Vera Allinson and H. Fowler Mear based on play by Cyril Campion	Arthur Houghton	Henry Edwards
	Doctor's Orders	Clifford Grey, R. P. Weston and Bert Lee based on story by Clifford Grey, Syd Courteney and Lola Harvey	Ronnie Blake	Norman Lee
	Those Were the Days	Fred Thompson, Frank Lauder and Frank Miller adapted from *The Magistrate* by Arthur Wing Pinero	Dickie	Thomas Bentley
	Blind Justice	Vera Allison based on play *Recipe for Murder* by Arnold Ridley	Ralph Summers	Bernard Vorhaus
1935	Brown on Resolution (Retitled: *Forever England* US titles: *Born for Glory* and *Torpedo Raider*)	J. O. C. Orton, Michael Hogan and Gerard Fairlie based on novel by C. S. Forester	Able Seaman Albert Brown	Walter Forde
	Car of Dreams	Austin Melford based on *Mesauto* by Miklos Vitez and Laszlo Vadnai	Robert Miller	Graham Cutts and Austin Melford
	Royal Cavalcade	Val Gielgud, Holt Marvell and Marjorie Deans	Boy	Thomas Bentley, Herbert Brenon, Norman Lee and Walter Summers
	Charing Cross Road	Con West and Clifford Grey based on radio play by Gladys and Clay Keyes	Tony	Albert de Courville
1936	First Offence (US title: *Bad Blood*)	Austin Melford based on story by Stafford Dickens	Johnnie Penrose	Herbert Mason
	Tudor Rose (US title: *Nine Days a Queen*)	Miles Malleson based on story by Robert Stevenson	Lord Guilford Dudley	Robert Stevenson
1937	O.H.M.S. (US title: *You're in the Army Now*)	Bryan Edgar Wallace, Austin Melford and A. R. Rawlinson based on story by Lesser Samuels and Ralph Gilbert Bettinson	Bert Dawson	Raoul Walsh

DATE	FILM	SCREENPLAY	ROLE	DIRECTOR
	The Green Cockatoo (US title: *Four Dark Hours*)	Edward Berkman based on original story and scenario by Graham Greene	Jim Connor	William Cameron Menzies
1939	Goodbye Mr Chips	R. C. Sherriff, Claudine West and Eric Maschwitz based on novel by James Hilton	Peter Colley	Sam Wood
1940	All Hands	Johnny Paddy Carstairs	Sailor	John Paddy Carstairs
1941	Old Bill and Son	Bruce Bairnsfather and Ian Dalrymple based on cartoons by Bruce Bairnsfather	Young Bill Busby	Ian Dalrymple
	Cottage to Let (US title: *Bombsight Stolen*)	Anatole de Grunwald and J. O. C. Orton adapted from play by Geoffrey Kerr	Flight-Lieutenant Perry	Anthony Asquith
1942	The Young Mr Pitt	Sidney Gilliatt and Frank Lauder	William Wilberforce	Carol Reed
	In Which We Serve	Noël Coward	'Shorty' Blake	Noël Coward and David Lean
	The Black Sheep of Whitehall	Angus MacPhail and John Dighton	Bobby	Will Hay and Basil Dearden
	The Big Blockade	Angus MacPhail		Charles Frend
1943	We Dive at Dawn	J. B. Williams and Val Valentine	Lieutenant Taylor, R.N.	Anthony Asquith
1944	Victory Wedding		Soldier	Jessie Matthews
	This Happy Breed	David Lean, Ronald Neame and Anthony Havelock-Allan based on play by Noël Coward	Billy Mitchell	David Lean
1945	Total War in Britain	Ritchie Calder and Miles Tomalin	Narrator	Paul Rotha
	Waterloo Road	Sidney Gilliat based on story by Val Valentine	Jim Colter	Sidney Gilliat
	The Way to the Stars (US title: *Johnny in the Clouds*)	Terence Rattigan based on story by Terence Rattigan and Anatole de Grunwald	Peter Penrose	Anthony Asquith
1946	Land of Promise	Ara Calder-Marshall, Miles Malleson, Wolfgang Wilhelm and Miles Tomalin	Narrator	Paul Rotha
	Great Expectations	David Lean and Ronald Neame based on novel by Charles Dickens	Pip	David Lean
1947	So Well Remembered	John Paxton based on novel by James Hilton	George Boswell	Edward Dymtryk
	The October Man	Eric Ambler	Jim Ackland	Roy Baker
1948	Scott of the Antarctic	William Meade and Ivor Montagu	Captain Robert Falcon Scott	Charles Frend
1949	The History of Mr Polly	Anthony Pelissier based on novel by H. G. Wells	Alfred Polly	Anthony Pelissier
	Friend of the Family	James Hill	Narrator	James Hill

DATE	FILM	SCREENPLAY	ROLE	DIRECTOR
	The Flying Skyscraper		Narrator	
	The Rocking Horse Winner	Anthony Pelissier based on short story by D. H. Lawrence	Bassett	Anthony Pelissier
1950	Morning Departure (US title: *Operation Disaster*)	William Fairchild based on play by Kenneth Woolard	Lieutenant Commander Armstrong	Roy Baker
1951	Mr Denning Drives North	Alec Coppel based on his own novel	Tom Denning	Anthony Kimmins
1952	The Gentle Gunman	Roger MacDougall based on his own play	Terence Sullivan	Basil Dearden
1953	The Long Memory	Robert Hamer and Frank Harvey based on novel by Winston Clewes	Davidson	Robert Hamer
1954	Hobson's Choice	David Lan, Norman Spencer and Wynyard Browne based on play by Harold Brighouse	Willie Mossop	David Lean
1955	The Colditz Story	Guy Hamilton, Ivan Foxwell and William Douglas Home based on book by P. R. Reid	Pat Reid	Guy Hamilton
	The End of the Affair	Leonore Coffee based on novel by Graham Greene	Albert Parkis	Edward Dymtryk
	Above Us the Waves	Robert Estridge based on story by C. E. T. Warren and James Benson	Commander Fraser	Ralph Thomas
	Escapade	Gilbert Holland based on play by Roger MacDougall	John Hampden	Philip Leacock
1956	War and Peace	Bridget Boland, Robert Westerby, King Vidor, Mario Camerini, Ennio de Conci and Ivor Perilli based on novel by Leo Tolstoy	Platon	King Vidor and Mario Soldati
	It's Great to be Young	Ted Willis	Mr Dingle	Cyril Frankel
	The Baby and the Battleship	Jay Lewis, Gilbert Hackforth-Jones and Bryan Forbes based on novel by Anthony Thorne	'Puncher' Roberts	Jay Lewis
	Around the World in 80 Days	James Poe, S. J. Perelman and John Farrow based on novel by Jules Verne	Cabby	Michael Anderson
1957	Town on Trial	Robert Westerby and Ken Hughes	Superintendent Mike Haloran	John Guillermin
	The Vicious Circle (US title: *The Circle*)	Francis Durbridge based on his television play *The Brass Candlestick*	Dr Howard Latimer	Gerald Thomas
1958	Dunkirk	David Divine, W. P. Liscomb based on *Dunkirk* by Ewen Butler and J. S. Bradford	Corporal Tubby Binns	Leslie Norman
	Ice Cold in Alex (US title: *Desert Attack*)	T. J. Morrison and Christopher Landon based on novel by Christopher Landon	Captain Anson	J. Lee Thompson

DATE	FILM	SCREENPLAY	ROLE	DIRECTOR
	I Was Monty's Double (US title: *Hell, Heaven, or Hoboken*)	Bryan Forbes based on book by M. E. Clifton James	Major Hervey	John Guillermin
1959	Tiger Bay	John Hawkesworth and Shelley Smith based on *Rudolphe et le Revolveur* by Noël Calef	Superintendent Graham	J. Lee Thompson
1960	Summer of the Seventeenth Doll (US title: *Season of Passion*)	John Dighton based on play by Ray Lawler	Barney	Leslie Norman
	The Swiss Family Robinson	Lowell S. Hawley based on novel by Johann Wyss	Father Robinson	Ken Annakin
	Tunes of Glory	James Kennaway based on his novel	Lieutenant-Colonel Basil Barrow	Ronald Neame
1961	The Singer Not the Song	Nigel Balchin based on novel by Audrey Erskine Lindop	Father Keogh	Roy Baker
1962	Flame in the Streets	Ted Willis adapted from his play *Hot Summer Night*	'Jacko' Palmer	Roy Baker
	The Valiant (Italian title: *L'Affondamento della 'Valiant'*)	Willis Hall and Keith Waterhouse based on play *L'Équipage au Complet* by Robert Mallet	Captain Morgan	Roy Baker
	Tiara Tahiti	Geoffrey Cotterell and Ivan Foxwell based on novel by Geoffrey Cottrell	Lientenant-Colonel Clifford Southey	William T. Kotcheff
1964	The Chalk Garden	John Michael Hayes based on play by Enid Bagnold	Maitland	Ronald Neame
1965	The Truth About Spring (TV title: *The Pirates of Spring Cove*)	James Lee Barrett based on *Satan* by Henri deVere Stacpole	Tommy Tyler	Richard Thorpe
	King Rat	Bryan Forbes based on novel by James Clavell	Smedley-Taylor	Bryan Forbes
	Operation Crossbow (US title: *The Great Spy Mission*)	Richard Imrie, Derry Quinn and Ray Digby	General Boyd	Michael Anderson
	The Wrong Box	Larry Gelbart, Bert Shevelove suggested story by Robert Louis Stevenson and Lloyd Osbourne	Masterman Finsbury	Bryan Forbes
	Sky West and Crooked* (US title: *Gypsy Girl*)	Mary Hayley Bell and John Prebble		John Mills
1967	The Family Way	Bill Naughton, adapted by Roy Boulting and Jeffrey Dell based on play *All in Good Time* by Bill Naughton	Ezra Fitton	Roy Boulting
	Chuka	Richard Jessup	Colonel Stuart Valois	Gordon Douglas
	Africa — Texas Style	Andy White	Wing-Commander Howard Hayes	Andrew Morton

DATE	FILM	SCREENPLAY	ROLE	DIRECTOR
1969	Run Wild, Run Free	David Rook based on his novel *The White Colt*	The Moorman	Richard C. Sarafian
	Oh! What a Lovely War	Len Deighton from Joan Littlewood's stage production based on *The Long Trail* by Charles Chilton	Field Marshal Sir Douglas Haigh	Richard Attenborough
	La Morte non ha Sesso (English title: *A Black Veil for Lisa*)	Giuseppe Belli, Vitoriano Petrilli, Massimo Dallamano and Audrey Nohra	Inspector Franz Bulov	Massimo Dallamano
	Lady Hamilton — Zwischen Smach und Liebe (English title: *Emma Hamilton*)	Werner P. Zibaso, Jameson Brewer and Christian Jaque based on novel by Alexandre Dumas	Sir William Hamilton	Christian Jaque
1970	Adam's Woman	Richard Fielder based on story by Lowell Barrington	Sir Philip McDonald	Philip Leacock
	Ryan's Daughter	Robert Bolt	Michael	David Lean
1971	Dulcima	Frank Nesbitt based on story by H. E. Bates	Mr Parker	Frank Nesbitt
	Young Winston	Carl Foreman based on *My Early Life* by Winston Churchill	General Kitchener	Richard Attenborough
1972	Lady Caroline Lamb	Robert Bolt	Canning	Robert Bolt
1973	Oklahoma Crude	Marc Norman	Cleon Doyle	Stanley Kramer
1976	Trial by Combat (US title: *Dirty Knights' Work*)	Julian Bond, Steven Rossen and Mitchell Smith based on story by Fred Weintraub and Paul Heller	Bertie Cook	Kevin Conor
1977	The Devil's Advocate	Morris West based on his novel	Blaise Meredith	Guy Green
1978	The Big Sleep	Michael Winner based on novel by Raymond Chandler	Inspector Jim Carson	Michael Winner
	The Thirty-Nine Steps	Michael Robson based on novel by John Buchan	Colonel Scudder	Don Sharp
1979	Zulu Dawn	Cy Endfield and Anthony Storey	Sir Henry Bartle Frere	Douglas Hickox
1981	Gandhi	John Briley	The Viceroy	Richard Attenborough
1983	Sahara	James R. Silke based on story by Menahem Golen	Cambridge	Andrew V. McLaglen
1987	When the Wind Blows	Raymond Briggs	James (voice only)	Jimmy T. Murakami
	Who's That Girl?	Andrew Smith and Ken Finkleman	Montgomery Bell	James Foley

Sky West and Crooked. John Mills only directed the film. He did not appear in it.

DATE	TITLE	WRITER	ROLE	DIRECTOR	COMPANY
1956	The Letter	Somerset Maugham	Robert Crosbie	William Wyler	American
1962	The Interrogator		British Officer		American
1967	Dundee and the Culhane		Dundee		American
1970	Nanny and the Professor		Busker		American
1973	The Zoo Gang	Reginald Rose, Howard Dimsdale, John Kruse, William Fairchild, Peter Yeldham and Sean Graham based on book by Paul Galico	Tommy Devon	Sidney Havers and John Hough	ATV
1978	Dr Strange	Phil de Guere based on *Marvel Comics* characters created by Stan Lee	Lidmer	Phil de Guere	CBS
1979	Quatermass	Nigel Kneale	Quatermass	Piers Haggard	Euston
1980	Galloping Foxley	Roald Dahl dramatized by Robin Chapman	William Perkins	Claude Whatham	Anglia
	Young at Heart	Vince Powell	Albert Collyer	Stuart Allen	ATV
	The Umbrella Man	Roald Dahl adapted by Ronald Harwood	The Man	Claude Whatham	Anglia
1981	Young at Heart	Vince Powell	Albert Collyer	Stuart Allen	ATV
1982	Operation Safecrack	Henry Sleser dramatized by Robin Chapman	Sam Morrisey	Alan Gibson	Anglia
	Young at Heart	Vince Powell	Albert Collyer	Stuart Allen	ATV
	The Adventures of Little Lord Fauntleroy	Blanche Hanakis	Earl of Doricourt	Desmond Davis	CBS
1984	The Masks of Death	N. J. Crisp from story by John Elder based on characters created by Sir Arthur Conan Doyle	Dr Watson	Roy Ward Baker	Channel 4
1985	A Woman of Substance	Lee Langley adapted from novel by Barbara Taylor Bradford	Henry Rossiter	Don Sharp	Channel 4
	Murder with Mirrors	George Eckstein based on novel by Agatha Christie	Lewis Serrocold	Dick Lowry	CBS
1987	Hold the Dream	Barbara Taylor Bradford	Henry Rossiter	Don Sharp	Channel 4
	Best of British	Maurice Sellar and Lou Jones	Narrator	Maurice Sellar and Robert Sedaway	
1988	80 Years On		Interview		BBC

DATE	TITLE	WRITER	ROLE	DIRECTOR	COMPANY
	Spit MacPhee	Moya Wood adapted from novel by James Aldridge	Fyfe MacPhee	Marcus Cole	Australia
1989	A Tale of Two Cities	Arthur Hopcroft adapted from novel by Charles Dickens	Jarvis Lorry	Philippe Monnier	Granada
1990	Ending Up	Douglas Livingstone based on novel by Kingsley Amis	Bernard	Peter Sasdy	Thames
	The George Cross — Beyond the Call of Death		Narrator	Michael Kerr	BBC
	Night of the Fox	Bennett Cohen based on novel by Jack Higgins	General Munro	Charles Jarrott	ITC
1992	Perfect Scoundrels	Peter J. Hammond	Praeger	Graham Theakston	ITV
1993	Frankenstein — The Real Story	David Wicks adapted from novel by Mary Shelley	de Lacey	David Wicks	Thames
	Harnessing Peacocks	Andrew Davies based on novel by Mary Wesley	Bernard	James Cellan Jones	ITV

RADIO

All productions for the BBC

1936	Entertainment Parade	1951	Concerning the English Desert Island Discs	1974	The Good Companions (extract)
1941	Women at War			1975	A History of Revue
1942	Annette Mills and her Songs	1952	She Stoops to Conquer	1982	Big Hearted Arthur
1949	Duet for Two Hands Hi Gang	1960	The John Mills Story	1983	David Niven
1950	Fire on the Snow	1973	Desert Island Discs	1986	The Petition (extract)

Acknowledgments

The author would like to begin by expressing his appreciation to Sir John Mills for his support and for allowing him access to his files.

The author would also like to thank Mark Collins, Cameron Brown, Colin Ziegler, Roger Bristow and Oliver Smee.

The author and publisher would like to express their appreciation to the following for their assistance and/or permission in relation to the following photographs: AB-Pathé 87; ABP 93, 96; Anglia Television Limited 138; BHP 109 (top); BIP 24; BL/Jambox 115; British Lion 30 (bottom), 81, 82, 83, 88 (top); Carlo Ponti/Dino de Laurentis 88 (bottom); Columbia 84, 90, 112, 114, 117, 124, 130; Daily Mail 143; Zoe Dominic 131; Ealing Films 46, 54, 65; EMI 120, 126, 127; FD/Ealing 75; Friday Productions 147; Gainsborough 31, 34, 49; Gaumont 14, 20, 21, 28, 30 (top), 35; GFD/Gainsborough 55, 57; GFD/Two Cities 56, 63, 66; John Haynes 128; Hulton Picture Library 17, 72; Legeran Films 48 (bottom); London Films 74; The Raymond Mander and Joe Mitchenson Theatre Collection 10; MGM 45, 113, 122; MGM/Ealing 95; Sir John Mills Collection 1, 6, 18, 19, 25, 26, 33, 36, 38, 39, 41, 42, 43, 44, 50, 58, 67, 68, 73, 97, 98, 106, 117 (top), 123, 133 (left and right), 136, 139, 141, 142, 144 (top and bottom), 145, 148; The National Film Archive 14, 20, 21, 22 (top and bottom), 23, 24, 28, 30 (top and bottom), 31, 34, 35, 37, 45, 48 (top and bottom), 51, 53, 54, 55, 56, 57, 59, 60, 61, 63, 65, 66, 71, 74, 75, 77, 81, 84, 85, 86, 87, 88 (top and bottom), 90, 92, 93, 95, 96, 100, 101, 102, 103, 104, 107, 108, 109 (top), 110, 111, 112, 113, 114, 115, 116, 117 (bottom), 119, 120, 122, 124, 126, 127, 130, 134; New World 37; Paramount Pictures Limited 116, 119; Pinnacle 86; Portsmouth Publishing and Printing 140; The Rank Organization 2, 60, 61, 71, 77, 85, 104, 107, 108; Rank /Two Cities 53; Real Art 22 (bottom); RKO/Alliance 62; Romulus 92; Samarkand 134; Thames Television 135, 146; Times Newspapers Limited 16, 132; Twentieth Century-Fox 51; Two Cities 59; United Artists 100; UA/Knightsbridge 102, 103; UA/Michael Todd 89; UA/Quota Rentals 110, 111; Walt Disney 101.

The author would like to add a personal note of thanks to Charles Merullo and also to John Haynes, Peter Hirst, M. Roffey, Alison Rogers, Lynne Willis, staff at the Theatre Museum and everybody at the BFI reference library and stills library.

159

Index

Above Us the Waves 11, 85
Adam's Woman 124
Adventures of Little Lord Fauntleroy, The 13
Affondamento della 'Valiant', L' 108
Africa – Texas Style 12
All Hands 48
All In Good Time 115
Aren't Men Beasts? 32
Around the World in Eighty Days 12, 89
At The End of The Day 9, 129

Baby and the Battleship, The 11, 89
Bad Blood 31
Big Sleep, The 13
Black Sheep of Whitehall, The 54
Bombsight Stolen 48
Born to Glory 29
Britannia of Billingsgate 21
Brown on Resolution 10, 29

Car of Dreams 31
Cavalcade 8, 18
Chalk Garden, The 12, 110
Charing Cross Road 31
Charles Cochrane's 1931 Revue 8
Charley's Aunt 8, 9, 17, 78
Chuka 12, 116
Circle, The 92
Colditz Story, The 11, 83
Cottages to Let 48

Desert Attack 96
Devil's Advocate, The 13, 133
Dr Strange 13
Duet for Two Hands 9, 59
Dulcima 13, 127
Dundee and the Culhane 13
Dunkirk 11, 94

Emma Hamilton 12, 116
End of the Affair, The 12, 84
Ending Up 13, 147
Escapade 11, 86
Evening with John Mills, An 10

Family Way, The 12, 115
Figure of Fun 9, 72
First Offence 31
Five O'Clock Girl, The 8
Flame in the Streets 12, 107
Floodlight 36
Forever England 10, 29
Four Dark Hours 36
Frankenstein, The Real Story 13

Galloping Foxley 139
Gandhi 13
Gentle Gunman, The 11, 75
Ghost Camera, The 23
Give Me A Ring 8
Good Companions, The 9, 130
Goodbye Mr Chips 9, 45, 140
Great Expectations 9, 10, 60
Great Spy Mission, The 112
Green Cockatoo, The 36

Hamlet 8
Harnessing Peacocks 13, 147
Hell, Heaven, or Hoboken 92
History of Mr Polly, The 11, 66
Hobson's Choice 11, 80
Hot Summer Night 107

I Was Monty's Double 11, 92
Ice Cold in Alex 11, 96
In Which We Serve 10, 52
It's Great To Be Young 11, 86

Jill Darling 8, 24
Journey's End 8

King Rat 12, 112

Lady Caroline Lamb 127
Lady Hamilton – Zwischen Smach und Liebe 116
Lash, The 23
Letter, The 13
Little Lies 9, 140
London Wall 8, 17
Long Memory, The 11, 76

Magistrate, The 9, 24, 140
Men in Shadow 9, 50
Midshipmaid, The 10, 21
Midshipmaid Gob 21
Midsummer Night's Dream, A 7, 8, 40
Morning Departure 11, 70
Mr Cinders 8
Mr Denning Drives North 11, 75

Nanny and the Professor, The 13
Nine Days a Queen 35

October Man, The 11, 63
Of Mice and Men 9, 45
Oh! What A Lovely War 12, 118
O.H.M.S. 35
Oklahoma Crude 13, 130
Old Bill and Son 48
Operation Crossbow 112
Operation Disaster 70

Pélissier's Follies 38
Perfect Scoundrels 13
Petition, The 9, 143
Pirates of Spring Cove, The 110
Power of Persuasion 9, 108
Pygmalion 10, 144

Quatermass 13, 135

Red Night 8, 32
River Wolves 23
Rocking Horse Winner, The 11, 67
Ross 9, 107
Run Wild, Run Free 12, 117
Ryan's Daughter 13, 123

Sahara 13
Scott of the Antarctic 11, 64
Season of Passion 101
Separate Tables 9, 132
She Stoops To Conquer 8, 43
Singer Not the Song, The 12, 105

Sky West and Crooked 12
So Well Remembered 11, 63
Spit McPhee 13, 144
Summer of the Seventeenth Doll 12, 101
Swiss Family Robinson, The 12, 101

Tale of Two Cities, A 13, 144
Tales of the Unexpected 13, 139
Thirty-Nine Steps, The 13, 133
This Happy Breed 10, 56
Those Were the Days 24
Tiara Tahiti 12, 108
Tiger Bay 12, 97
Top of the Ladder 9, 72
Torpedo Raider 29
Town on Trial 11, 91
Truth About Spring, The 12, 110
Tudor Rose 35
Tunes of Glory 12, 102

Uninvited Guest, The 9, 78

Valiant, The 12, 108
Veterans 9, 128
Vicious Circle, The 11, 92

War and Peace 12, 89
Waterloo Road 8, 10, 57
Way to the Stars, The 10, 59
We at the Crossroads 9
We Dive at Dawn 10, 55
Who's That Girl? 13, 143
Words and Music 8, 18
Wrong Box, The 12, 114

Young at Heart 13, 139
Young Mr Pitt, The 50
Young Winston 13, 124
Young Woodley 8
You're in the Army Now 35

Zoo Gang, The 13
Zulu Dawn 13, 135